Mel Bay Presents

Aaron Shearer

Learning the Classic Guitar

Part Two

With music composed by Alan Hirsh

Edited by Tom Poore

Learning the Classic Guitar Part One and *Part Two* were written to be used together. Both volumes are available from your local music dealer or from Mel Bay Publications, Inc.

1 2 3 4 5 6 7 8 9 0

Visit us on the Web at www.melbay.com — E-mail us at email@melbay.com

Contents

Introduction

Part Two: Reading Music should be used concurrently with *Part One: Technique*. The music in this book is written to conform to a gradual development of both technique and reading music. Since counting rhythms is often the main weakness among students, this aspect of development is emphasized.

Each solo and duet are credited with the initials of its composer: "A.H." for Alan Hirsh, and "A.S." for Aaron Shearer. Joint efforts are marked with "S-H."

Left-hand fingering numbers are generally placed to the left of the note head — slightly above the treble part, slightly below the bass part, and level with notes which appear within a chord. One exception is when the finger is to be held down while succeeding notes are played (indicated 1–, 2–, etc.), or when it must glide up the string (1↗) or down (1↘) to form a succeeding note. In these cases, it seems more appropriate to place the fingering number to the right of the note head.

Generally, fingering is kept to a minimum. Students should learn to read notes rather than fingering symbols. Further, students should learn to work out fingerings on their own — particularly in passages where there's only one practical fingering — and they should be encouraged to write their fingerings in the music.

Because of its gradual approach, *Part Two* is limited to basic training in the first position of the fingerboard. Higher positions and advanced techniques (barring, harmonics, vibrato, pizzicato, etc.), will be covered in future volumes of this series.

Alan Hirsh, guitarist and composer, was born in 1955 in Tucson, Arizona. He earned his bachelor's degree from the University of Arizona, where he studied composition with Robert Muczynski. He then earned his master's degree from the Peabody Conservatory of Music, where he studied with Vladimir Ussachevsky and Jean Eichelberger Ivey.

His solo and ensemble works for the guitar have been performed throughout the United States and abroad. He received the ASCAP Raymond Hubbel Award in 1979 and 1984, and the Otto Ortman Award from the Peabody Conservatory in 1982 and 1983.

Mr. Hirsh currently lives in Des Plaines, Illinois, where he works as music director at Lake Forest Academy. He is also completing his doctoral studies through the Peabody Conservatory.

Music and the Guitar

Learning the guitar and learning to read music are closely linked — neither can stand alone. Your progress in learning to play the guitar and your confidence as a performer will be directly related to your ability to read music.

You can best learn to securely read music through a gradual approach. You'll begin by acquiring a basic understanding of what music is and how it affects us.

The Five Basic Materials of Music

We're all aware that everyday sounds influence us powerfully. Pleasant, quiet sounds are soothing — sudden, raucous noises are disturbing. Music affects us similarly. Soft and regular sounds, gently rising or falling pitches, and consonant harmonies are calming — harsh and irregular sounds, sudden large skips of pitch, and dissonant harmonies are exciting. By mixing and contrasting these qualities, composers evoke a wide variety of emotional responses.

There are five basic materials of music:

Rhythm is the organization of sounds in time. Differences in the durations of sounds and in their frequency and regularity form rhythmic groups or figures. Irregular rhythms and rapid tempos create movement and activity — regular rhythms and slower tempos create rest and tranquility. The interaction of contrasting rhythms gives music its rhythmic vitality. Further, a composition's expressive character is powerfully influenced by rhythmic contrasts.

Melody is a musically coherent succession of single tones.[†] Generally, melody is the most important element of a composition — it's the part we most often remember and whistle or hum.

Harmony is the blending of two or more tones, as in a chord, arpeggio, or when the melody is accompanied by one or more parts. Harmonies can be consonant and restful, or dissonant and active. Interplay between consonance and dissonance gives music its harmonic contrast.

Dynamics refers to the relative loudness or softness of music. Dynamics strongly influence the effect of music on the listener. Depending on its loudness or softness, and how sudden or gradual are its dynamic changes, a musical passage can convey either excitement or tranquility.

[†]Throughout this book, "tone" refers to an actual sound; "note" refers to the written representation of a sound.

Timbre (French, pronounced "**tam**-bur") is tone color and refers to the various qualities of musical sound. For example, a note played on a violin sounds different from the same note played on a trumpet — the difference is in the timbre. Depending on its timbre, a sound may be beautiful and appealing or harsh and unpleasant. In the hands of an accomplished player, the guitar has a particularly broad range of timbres — terms like "mellow," "warm," "thin," and "metallic" are often used to describe these various timbres.

∾ ∾ ∾ ∾ ∾ ∾ ∾

Although these basic materials have been defined separately, each is influenced by the others. For example, your response to a melody is not only influenced by the melody's pitch and rhythms, but also by its accompanying harmonies, by its loudness or softness, and by its brightness or warmth of timbre.

Learning to Read Music

Now is the most important time in your training as a musician. The habits of thought and movement you're about to build will influence every aspect of your later development, including your ability to perform for others. Depending on how you study, you'll learn either habits of security and confidence or habits of insecurity and confusion. Careful study will bring you progress and success — careless study will bring you difficulty and disappointment.

You can build strong habits of security and confidence from the beginning as you learn to read and play music. Always apply the following guidelines as you work with this book:

- ***Carefully study the text. Understand as fully as possible what you're attempting to do.***
- ***Recognize and avoid confusion and error. If you're having difficulty with something, stop immediately. Clarify the problem and decide on a solution.***
- ***Be sure that you understand and can securely execute a section before moving on to another.***

To read and play music fluently, you must learn to react automatically to both rhythm and pitch notation. You'll begin with rhythm.

Rhythm

Rhythmic groups or figures are centered on pulsations of sound called ***beats.*** Each beat is either strong or weak, depending on its relative stress. You can feel the relationship of strong and weak beats by counting steadily in the following manner: "1, 2, 1, 2, 1, 2," etc. Notice that you tend to stress the count of 1 — this is the strong beat; 2 is the weak beat. Now count aloud the following: "1, 2, 3, 1, 2, 3, 1, 2, 3," etc. Again, notice that you tend to stress the count of 1 — this is the strong beat; 2 and 3 are the weak beats.

As you count, notice that these combinations of strong and weak beats tend to form groups of either twos or threes. In musical notation, these groups are marked off by bar lines which form measures:

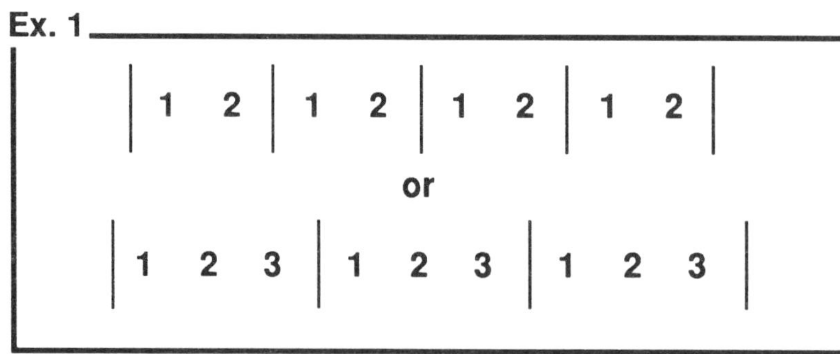

Directing the Beat

Most of us respond naturally to music which has a strong beat. We tend to nod or tap our feet in time with the beat. But although our response as listeners is automatic, creating a dependable beat as a performer requires considerable training.

Counting the beat aloud is an essential first step toward establishing a secure habit of counting. By itself, however, counting aloud isn't enough — you need to feel the beat through larger and more distinct movements. You can accomplish this with large and well-defined movements of your right arm. This is called ***directing the beat,*** and it's done in the following manner:

- ❑ **Relax your right upper arm, letting it rest at your side.**
- ❑ **With your hand half closed, rest your thumb against your index finger.**
- ❑ **Bend your elbow sharply, so that your forearm is angled comfortably upward and your hand is in front of your shoulder. This is the starting position.**
- ❑ **Swing your forearm down to a horizontal position and stop sharply. This stop defines the instant of the beat.**
- ❑ **Swing your forearm up to the starting position and stop sharply. This stop evenly divides the time between beats.**

As you carry out Ex. 2, your down-up movements (indicated by the arrows) should be precise and quick enough to allow a slight pause between each movement. This gives you a clear and strong feeling of the beat. Count aloud as you practice directing the following beats and divisions:

Ex. 2

| 1 & 2 & | 1 & 2 & | 1 & 2 & | etc.
↓ ↑ ↓ ↑ ↓ ↑ ↓ ↑ ↓ ↑ ↓ ↑

| 1 & 2 & 3 & | 1 & 2 & 3 & | etc.
↓ ↑ ↓ ↑ ↓ ↑ ↓ ↑ ↓ ↑ ↓ ↑

Rhythm Notation

In music notation, a tone is represented by a ***note.*** A silence is represented by a ***rest.*** The duration of a note or rest is called its ***value.*** The following values are represented by the notes and rests indicated:

Quarter value: Both ♩ and ♩ are quarter notes; 𝄽 is a quarter rest.

Eighth value: Both ♪ and ♪ are eighth notes; 𝄾 is an eighth rest.

The eighth value is exactly half of one quarter value. Thus, ♪ ♪ equals ♩, and 𝄾 𝄾 equals 𝄽. When two eighth notes appear in succession, they're often beamed together: ♫ or ♫ .

Meter and Time Signature

The beat provides music with a constant pulse. ***Meter*** (sometimes spelled "metre") is the number of beats in a measure. The ***time signature*** indicates both the meter and the note value which defines one beat. The upper number indicates the number of beats per measure — the lower number indicates the note value which represents one beat.

The following are commonly found time signatures:

$\frac{2}{4}$: two beats to the measure; the quarter value defines the beat.

$\frac{3}{4}$: three beats to the measure; the quarter value defines the beat.

$\frac{4}{4}$: four beats to the measure; the quarter value defines the beat.

Musicians often refer to $\frac{2}{4}$ as duple meter, $\frac{3}{4}$ as triple meter, and $\frac{4}{4}$ as quadruple meter.

Since duple meter is the easiest to count, you'll begin with $\frac{2}{4}$. Practice Ex. 3 slowly enough to avoid confusion and error. Keep your arm movements crisp, even, and steady as you direct the beat. First count aloud: "1 & 2 &," etc. Then keep a steady count in your mind and say "tah" (**T**) *for the full duration of each note.*

Ex. 3

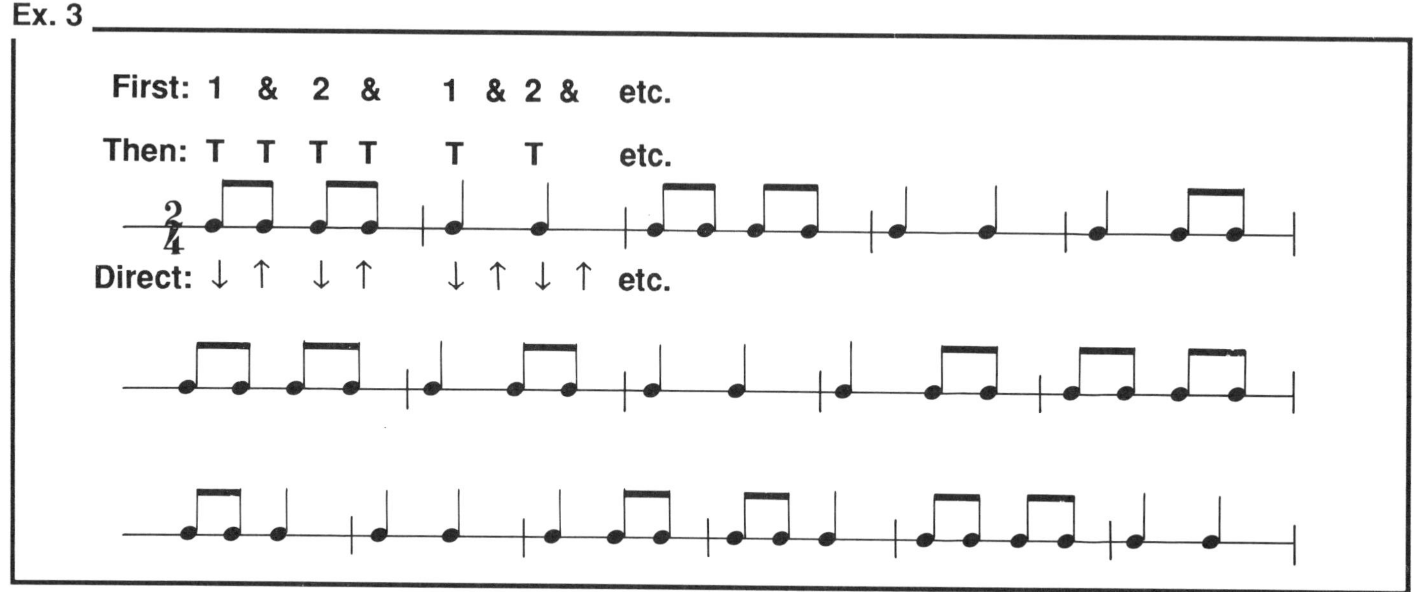

The ability to maintain a steady beat is extremely important. Try to develop a strong sense of rhythmic accuracy and steadiness. No one is born with this ability — you must acquire it through careful training.

Using the Metronome

The ***metronome,*** calibrated in clicks per minute, is invaluable for developing the ability to maintain a steady beat. In a musical score, the metronome is usually indicated as "M.M."

As you practice Exs. 4 – 8, set the metronome for one click per eighth note — one click for each ↓, and one click for each ↑. Choose a slow tempo at first, one which allows you to practice confidently and without error (approximately M.M. ♪ = 80). As you gain security, gradually increase the tempo until you can do the exercises at M.M. ♪ = 120.

After you've achieved this, reset the metronome to 60 (or even slower if necessary) and practice one quarter note ♩ (↓ ↑) or two eighth notes ♫ (↓ ↑) per click. Strongly emphasize the ↓ of "1" and "2." Gradually increase the tempo as you gain confidence.

Always remember, you can't learn accuracy by allowing confusion and error to creep into your practice. If you start making errors, or even feel that you might make errors, choose a slower tempo.

First practice counting and directing the entire exercise. Then use "tah" for the notes and count the rests.

Ex. 4

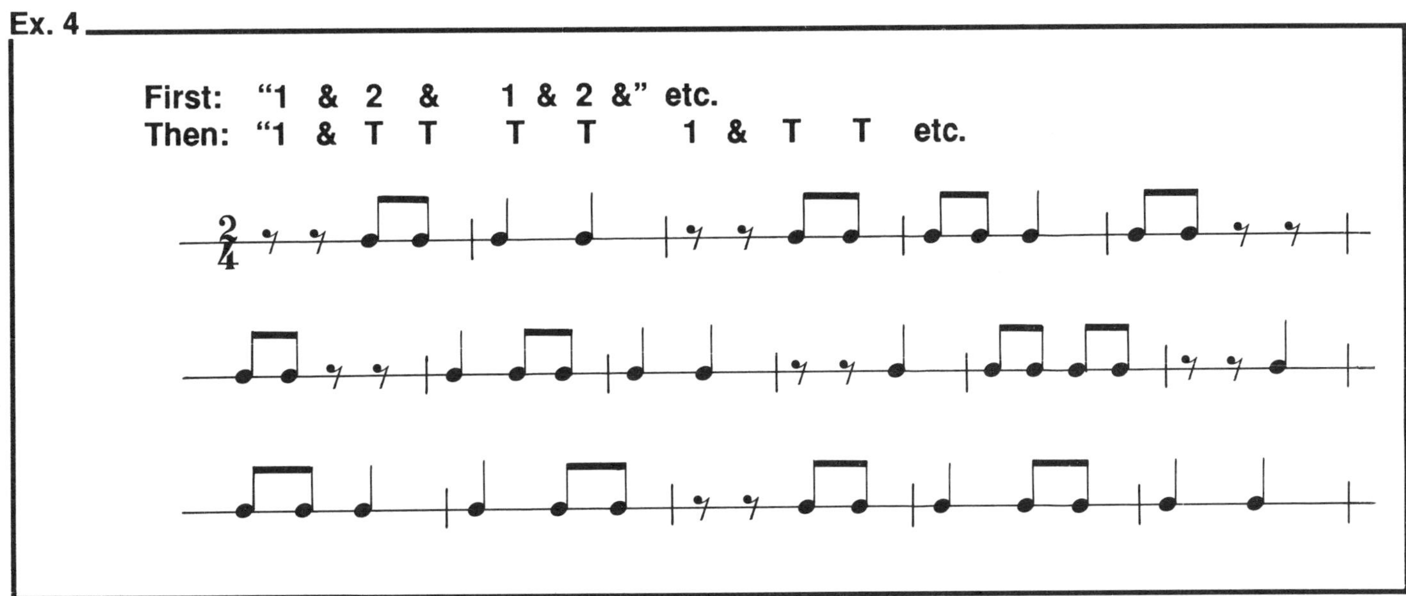

Ex. 5, with 𝄽 (Quarter Rests)

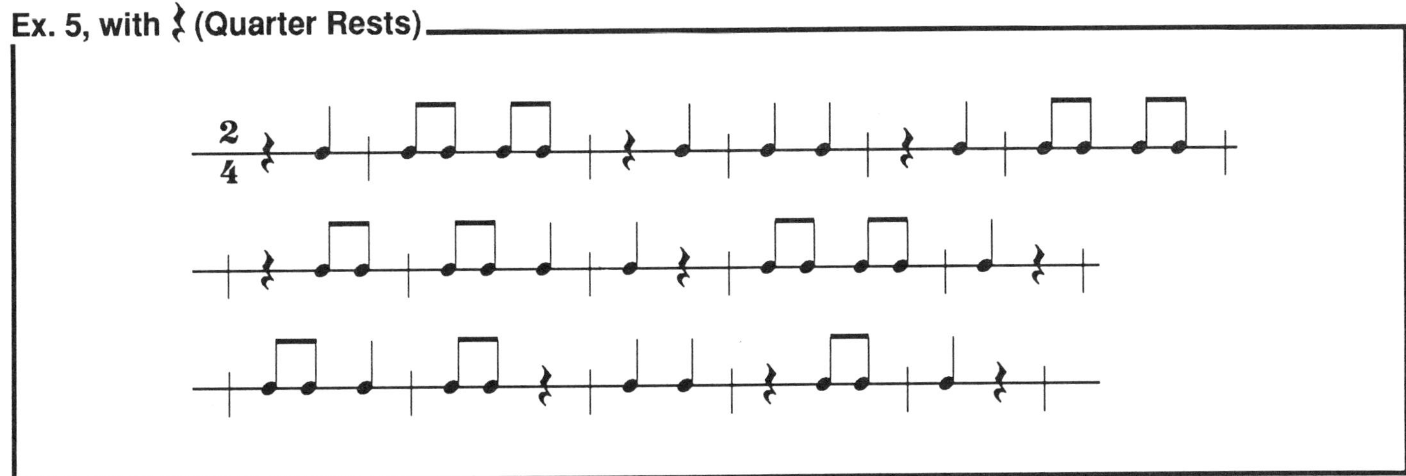

Ex. 6, with Notes Beginning on the Second Half (↑) of the Beat

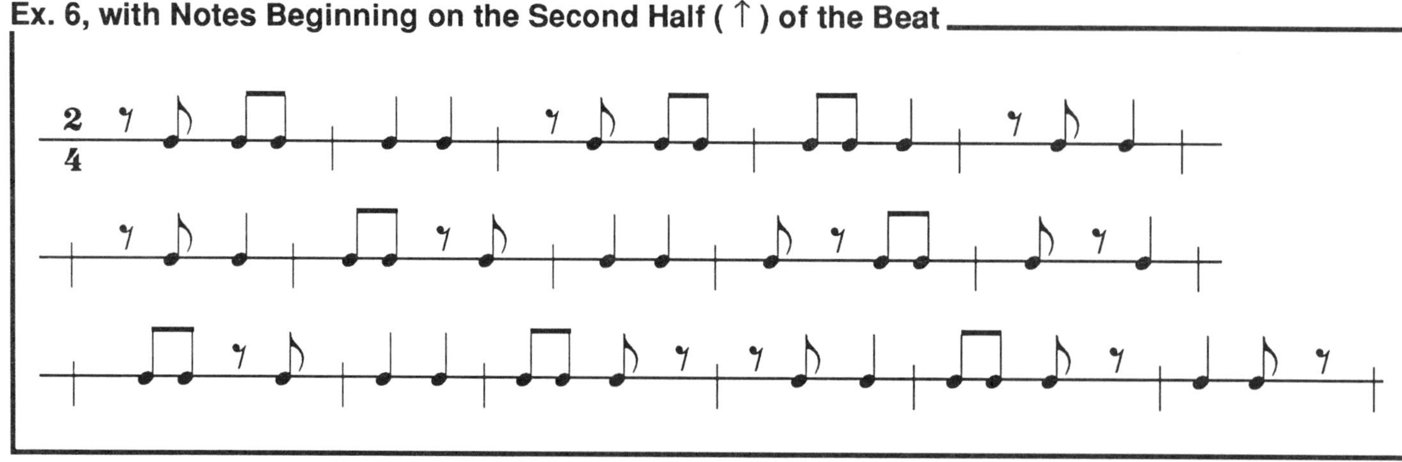

Composers generally use symbols as economically as possible. Thus, 𝄽 is almost always used in place of 𝄾𝄾 .

Ex. 7

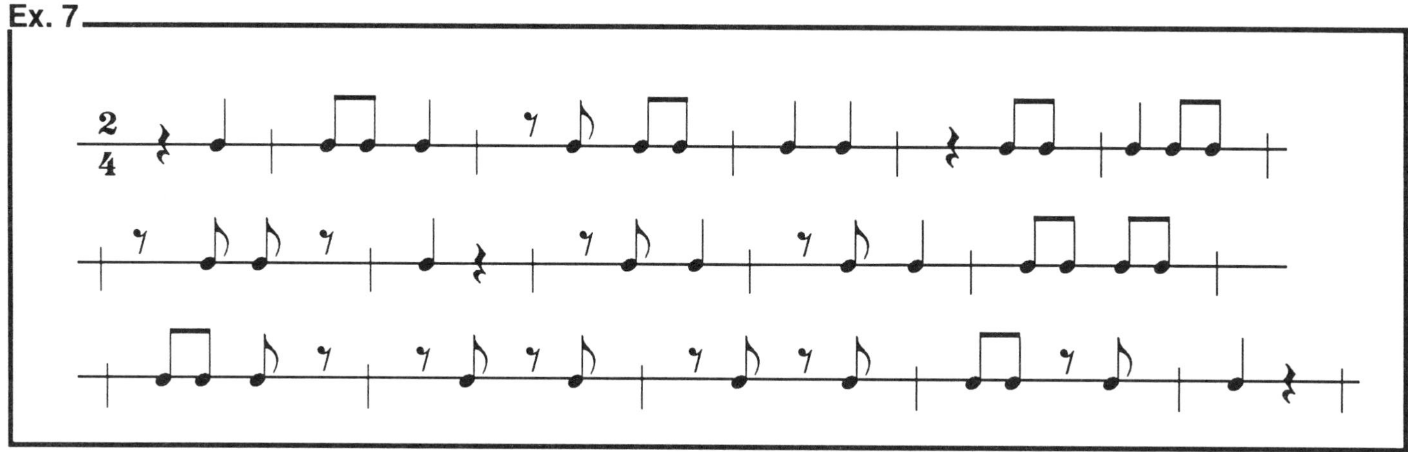

Although so far you've encountered only eighth notes beamed together in twos ♫ , eighth notes can also be beamed together in threes and fours .

Ex. 8

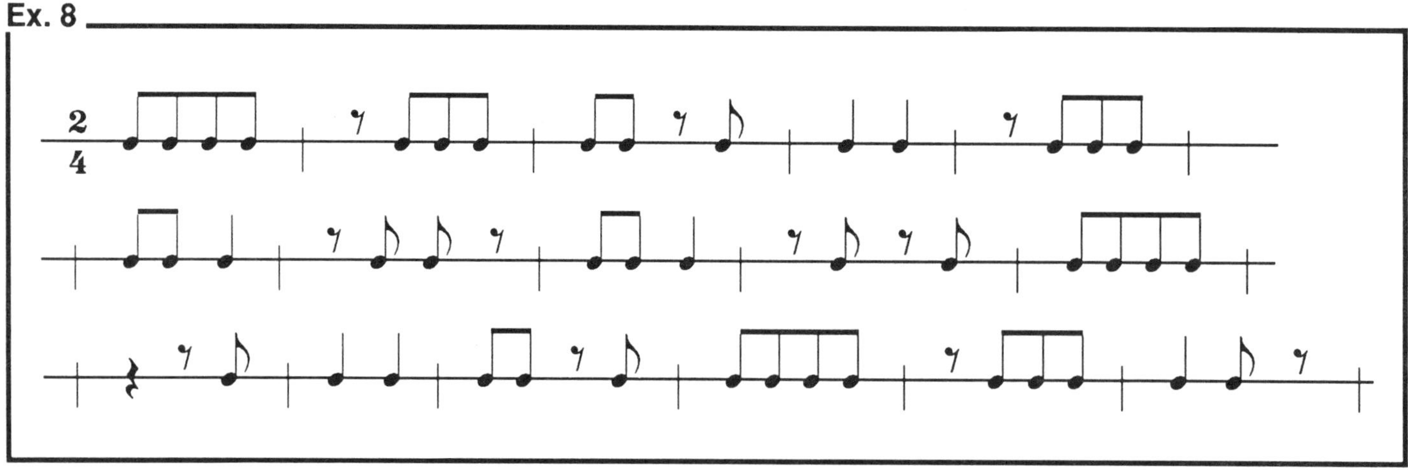

Are you making errors as you practice these exercises? Are you confused and hesitating? If so, slow down and practice the troublesome measures separately. When you've clarified and solved the problems, gradually increase the tempo.

Now is the time to acquire habits of accuracy, continuity, and confidence. By establishing these habits from the beginning, you're building a secure basis for reading and expressively playing music.

Directing the Beat with Your Foot

Directing the beat with your right arm is beneficial for studying music, but you obviously can't do this when you're playing the guitar. Thus, you must learn to carry out a similar down-up movement with your foot.

Proceed as follows, using whichever foot feels more comfortable as you play:

❑ **Begin by comfortably lifting only the ball of your foot — don't lift the heel. Then, directing the beat with your arm, move your foot down and up along with the movement of your arm. Remember, both the down and up movements are equally important, and they must be as precise with your foot as they are with your arm.**

❑ **Repeat Exs. 4 – 8, directing the beat with both your arm and your foot.**

❑ **When you feel confident with the preceding steps, repeat Exs. 4 – 8, directing the beat with only your foot.**

Pitch Notation

The five lines and four spaces which form the musical staff are the basis of pitch notation. Pitches above and below the staff are indicated with short lines called ***ledger lines.*** Ledger lines also form additional spaces above and below the staff.

Each line and space represents one of the seven letters of the musical alphabet: A, B, C, D, E, F, G. These letters correspond to the following solfege[†] syllables: La, Ti, Do, Re, Mi, Fa, So.

The ***treble clef*** appears at the beginning of the staff. Its scroll curls around the second line (G) — thus, this clef is also often called the ***G clef.***

[†]French, pronounced "sol-**feige**" as in "beige."

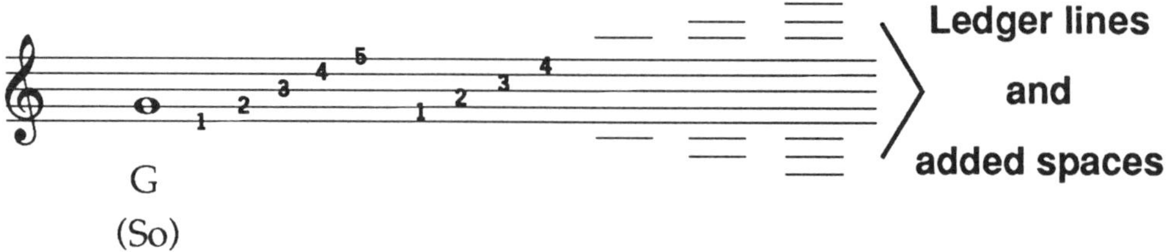

A gradual, step-by-step approach is the key to learning solfege easily and securely. In using this book, you'll learn the syllables and their locations on both the staff and the guitar. Also, since the use of letter names is so firmly established (especially in the English-speaking world), you should learn to identify each note by both its letter name and solfege syllable.†

†If you're an experienced guitarist and already read music, see pp. 209 – 211 for an explanation of solfege.

Beginning to Read and Play Music

Before you begin, make sure that your guitar is accurately tuned (see *Part One*, pp. x – xii). Also, carefully review the following points of technique:

- **Positioning the guitar (*Part One*, pp. 12 – 20)**
- **Right-hand positioning (*Part One*, pp. 33 – 36)**
- **Sounding the strings with p (*Part One*, pp. 37 – 42)**

The Open Third and Fourth Strings

A string which isn't being held against a fret is called an open string. The open third-string note is G (So). The open fourth-string note is D (Re). They're notated on the staff as follows:

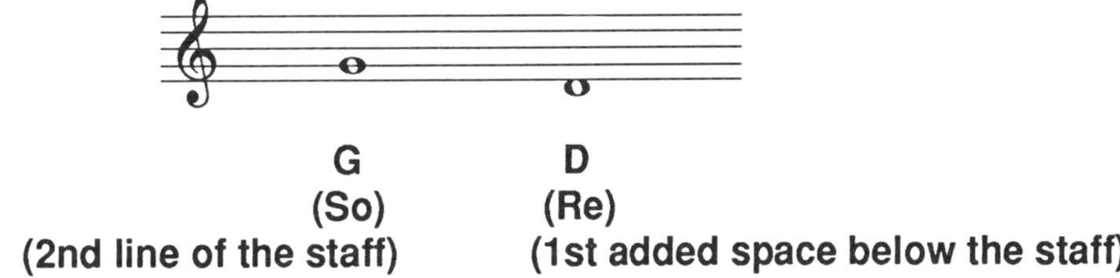

Using p, practice the following examples. Play slowly at first, keeping the correct hand position and movements. Then gradually quicken the tempo.

Now begin sounding alternate strings (Ex. 10). Again, start slowly, and continually check p to ensure that your position and movements are accurate. Then close your eyes and continue playing. Visualize the string and your movements — aim to see a clear image in your mind's eye as you sound the strings. Continue until you can confidently sound both strings without watching p.

Ex. 10

The Pre-Reading Procedure

You'll build secure habits of accuracy and confidence only through secure understanding. Your muscles can do only what your mind tells them to do, so you must have a clear direction before beginning to play. Thus, to progress quickly and avoid confusion and error, you must understand the music and know where the notes are found on the guitar.

Pre-reading is a systematic way to eliminate confusion before you attempt to play music.

Pre-reading is also an efficient and effective approach to developing secure and fluent sightreading. By solving problems before you actually play, you're doing essentially what proficient readers do at sight. The difference is in how quickly you do it: well-trained sightreaders read ahead and solve problems as they play — since you're still developing your reading ability, you'll solve problems more slowly and deliberately. By working in this manner, you'll build habits which will enable you to sightread with accuracy and confidence.

Pre-reading involves visualization, and visualization is the key to minimizing confusion and error. ***Visualization*** means reading the music away from the guitar — seeing the music unfold under your fingers as though you were actually playing it. The purpose of visualization is to ensure that you clearly understand the music *before* you attempt to play it.

The Pre-Reading Procedure is carried out in two steps — *without the guitar.*

• Step One: Clarify the Rhythms

Using a metronome, set the tempo as slow as necessary to avoid confusion and error. Go through the entire piece at least twice:

a. Count while directing the beat with your foot and right hand.

b. Vocalize the note values (using the neutral syllable "tah") while directing the beat.

Are you having trouble with any of the rhythms? If you are, isolate each problematic rhythm and practice until you can do it accurately. Then practice the entire piece — first counting, then vocalizing each value — until you're secure. If you have no problems with the rhythms, go on to Step Two.

• Step Two: Solfege Each Note and Visualize It on the Guitar

While directing the beat, sing the solfege syllable for each note — if you haven't acquired the ability to sing correct pitches at sight, say the syllables. Aim to clearly see in your mind's eye the note's exact location on the guitar. (Hereafter, "solfege" will always refer to the act of singing or saying solfege syllables.)

~ ~ ~ ~ ~ ~ ~

The importance of the Pre-Reading Procedure can't be overemphasized — it's the fastest and most secure way to learn to read and play music. Always carry out this procedure until you can do each step fluently and easily.

Duets for Study

The following duets will give you practice with basic rhythms and pitches. The upper part is for you, and the lower part is for your teacher or an experienced guitarist. Always thoroughly practice your part before playing it with another guitarist.

Carefully follow the Pre-Reading Procedure before you begin to play each duet. When you begin to play, continue directing the beat with your foot, and solfege each note as you play. If rhythm is a problem, count aloud as you play. Practice with the metronome, and go as slowly as necessary for accuracy. Practice each duet until you can play it accurately and confidently at about M.M.♩ = 63.

CAUTION: *When playing any music for the first time, always begin at a slow enough tempo to avoid confusion and error!* You should regard each metronome setting in this book as a goal to be achieved through careful pre-reading and practice.

Each of these duets ends with a ***dotted double bar*** (:‖); this means that the piece is to be repeated once.

So-Re One

Duet No. 1

A. S.

So-Re Two

Duet No. 2

A. S.

So-Re Three

Duet No. 3

A. S.

So-Re Four

Duet No. 4

S-H

So-Re Five

Duet No. 5 S-H

To the Teacher: Although string damping to observe rests and avoid dissonant overlapping of tones is an essential technique, no book can determine exactly when students should begin learning the various damping techniques. Students vary in their ability to handle string damping during their early development. Only you can determine when an individual student is ready. (For information on string damping, see pp. 206 – 208).

The Open Second String

The open second string is B (Ti), as indicated on this staff:

Ex. 11 uses all three of the open strings which you've studied so far. Again, start slowly, and continually check p to ensure that your position and movements are accurate. Then close your eyes and continue playing while visualizing the strings and your movements.

Ex. 11

Learn to avoid confusion and error. Always use the Pre-Reading Procedure before playing the following pieces. Also, continue to use the metronome during your practice.

Bugler's Tune

Solo No. 1

S-H

Melody

Duet No. 6

S-H

Rest and Play I

Duet No. 7

S-H

Note Values Longer than the Beat

Until now, you've only encountered values which equal one beat (♩ or 𝄽) or a half beat (♪ or 𝄾). But when the note value is longer than one beat, only the first beat of the note is clearly defined — the remaining beats must be clear in your mind as you count.

You'll begin with the simplest of longer values: the ***half value.*** The half note 𝅗𝅥 or half rest 𝄼 equals two beats, two quarter values, or four eighth values.

Count aloud while playing the following example:

Ex. 12

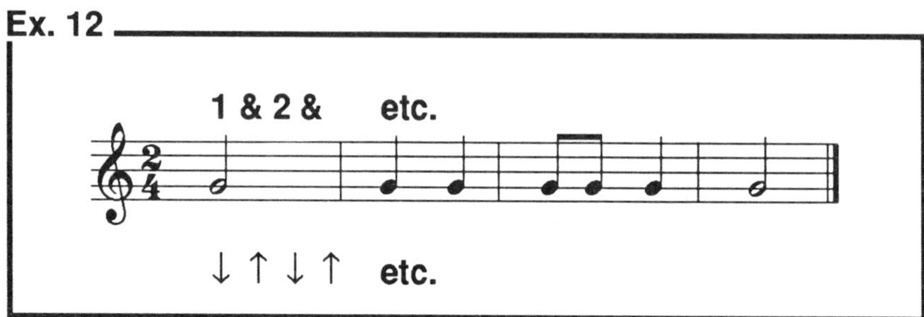

Different Endings of a Piece

Duet No. 8 introduces an important element of music notation: a ***first ending*** and a ***second ending.*** Each ending is identified by a bracket and the appropriate number — either 1. or 2. The first ending is played before repeating the piece (as indicated by the dotted double bar). After playing the piece a second time, you skip the first ending and play only the second ending.

In measure 9 of Duet No. 8, you'll encounter the ***whole-measure rest*** 𝄻 . For convenience, composers traditionally use this symbol to indicate a full measure of silence — regardless of the time signature.†

---

†Another use of this symbol is explained on p. 27.

Duet No. 8

Rest and Play II

S. H.

Notes on the Fingerboard

Before proceeding, carefully review "Beginning Left-Hand Training," *Part One*, pp. 43 – 48. You should also review the following notational symbols (see *Part One*, p. 29):

Circled numbers, ① ② ③ ④ ⑤ ⑥, indicate strings.

Uncircled numbers, 1, 2, 3, 4, indicate left-hand fingers. A zero indicates that no left-hand finger is used.

Roman numerals, I through XIX, indicate frets.

A (La) on ③

Form the note A by pressing ③ (third string) against II (second fret) with 2 (left-hand finger). Keep your fingertip very close to the fret.

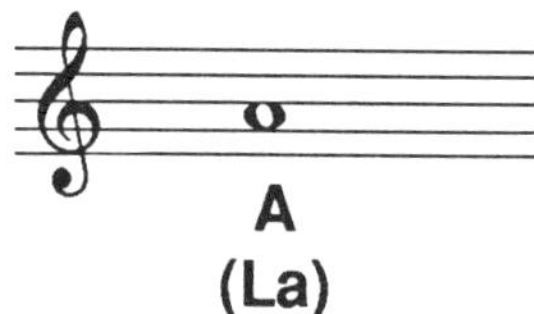

Visualizing Notes on the Fingerboard

To learn the notes on the fingerboard, begin by watching the fingerboard and your finger positions as you play. Solfege each note. Then close your eyes and continue to solfege and play. Visualize your finger movements as you play — aim to see each movement in your mind's eye.

Repeat each of the figures in the following example until you can play them accurately and confidently.

Ex. 13

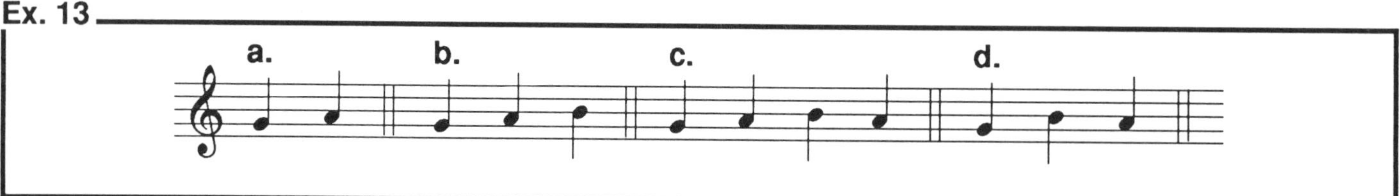

Until now, you've visualized only open strings during the Pre-Reading Procedure (see p. 12). The introduction of A (La) on II, however, requires you to do more than simply visualize the string. Thus, you now need to include a third step in the Pre-Reading Procedure:

• Step Three: Visualize Left-Hand Movements

a) Positively determine the string, the fret, and the left-hand fingering.

b) Solfege in correct rhythm as you direct the beat, visualizing each finger as though it's actually depressing the string against the fret.

∾ ∾ ∾ ∾ ∾ ∾ ∾

Using the three-step Pre-Reading Procedure, practice the following example:

Ex. 14

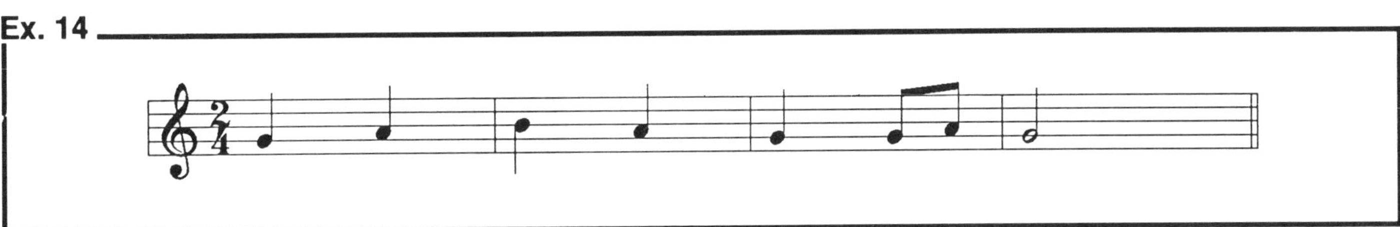

Remember, your hands are directed by your mind. It's essential that you carry out the Pre-Reading procedure *before practicing any new music*. You'll progress rapidly only if you thoroughly understand the music and how to play it. Acquire habits of accuracy and confidence. ***Avoid confusion and error!***

Lullaby

Duet No. 9

S-H

Dance of Four

Solo No. 2

S-H

C (Do) and D (Re) on ②

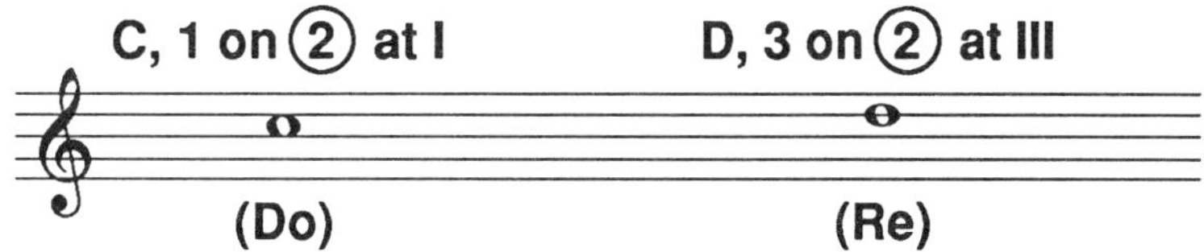

NOTE: If you can't comfortably reach D with 3, use 4.

Carefully practice each figure in the following example. When D (Re) follows C (Do), as in figures **b.** and **d.,** gently hold 1 against the string as you form D with 3. This gives an added sense of security for your left hand.

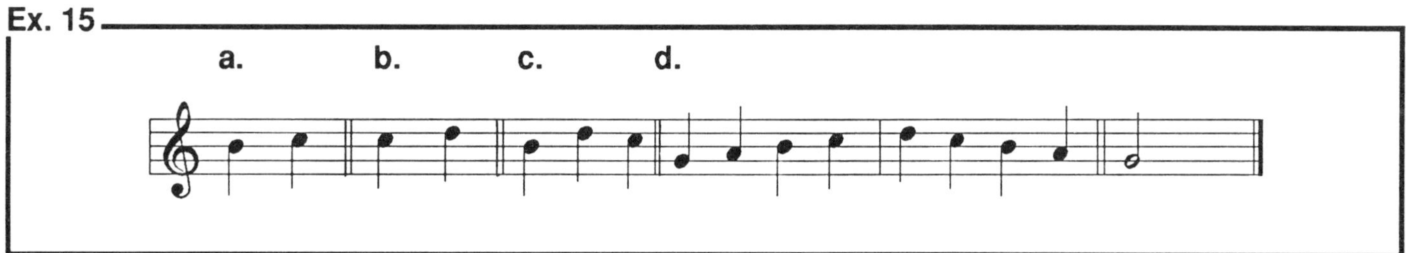

Have you thoroughly carried out the Pre-Reading Procedure? Have you clearly visualized the fingering as you played? Are you accurately and confidently solfeging each note? Don't rush through these examples — strive to understand the material as thoroughly as possible.

Scale Song

Duet No. 10

S-H

Solo No. 3

Dance of Six

A. H.

4/4 Time and the Whole Value

The whole note 𝅝 and the whole rest 𝄻 each equal two half values, or four quarter values, or eight eighth values. Thus, with ♩ representing one beat, whole notes and rests are counted as follows:

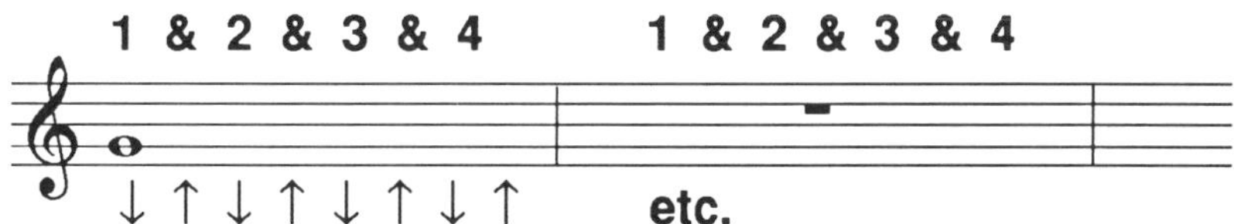

Since whole notes and rests require measures of at least four beats, you're now ready to practice the 4/4 time signature:

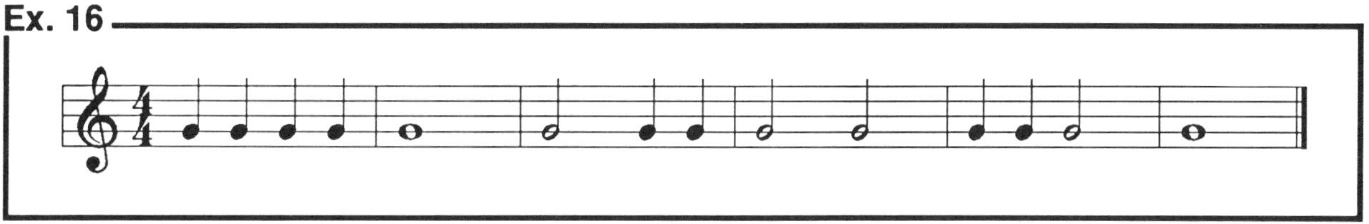

Duet No. 11

Counterpoint

S-H

4/4 time is so common in music that it's often called ***common time.*** Thus, composers often indicate 4/4 time with a **C** .

The Weaver

Duet No. 12

S-H

Solo No. 4 requires you to skip from ④ to ② with p. This upward skip should present little trouble, since p naturally moves in this direction after sounding a lower string.

Dance of the Upward Skip

Humming Song I

Duet No. 13a

2/2: Alla Breve

Although so far only the quarter value has been used to indicate the beat, the half value is also often used. The 2/2 time signature indicates that there are two half values to a measure and each half value receives one beat. This time signature is called ***alla breve*** (pronounced either "ah-lah **brev**" or "ah-lah **brev**-vay"). Less formally, 2/2 is also called ***cut time*** (common time cut in half), and is usually indicated with a ₵ .

When you direct the beat for cut time, ↓ and ↑ each defines one quarter value.

Ex. 17

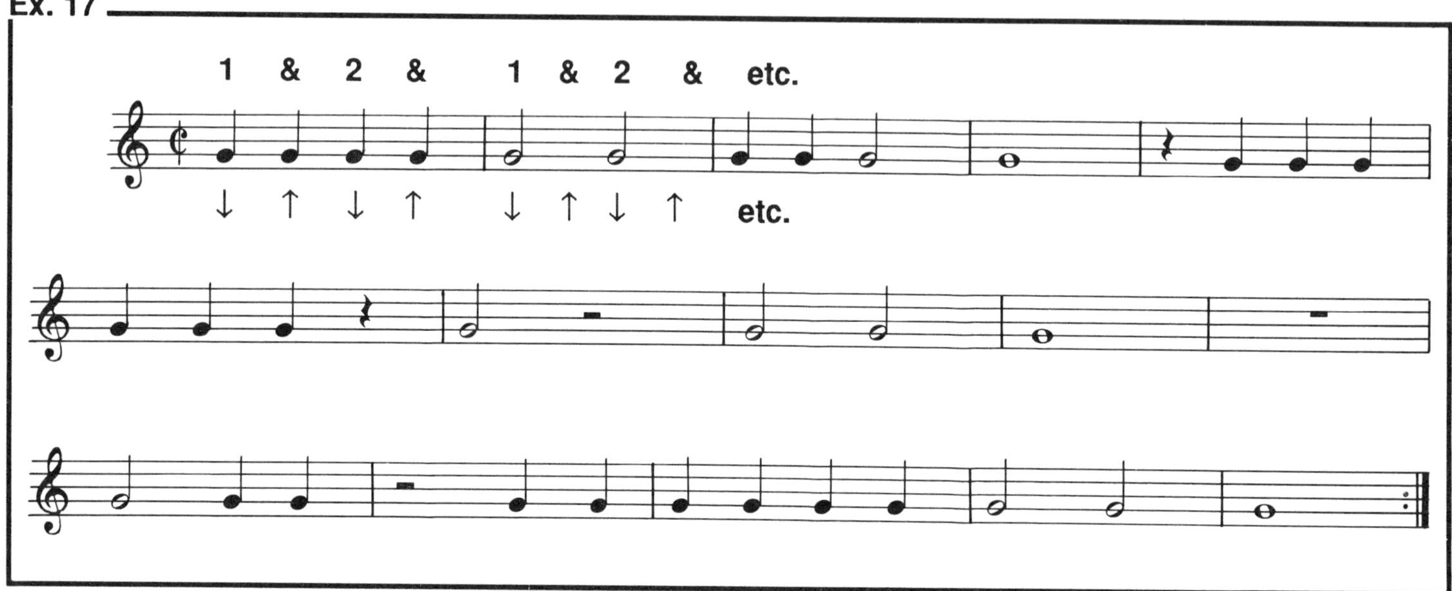

Notice that, when you maintain the same pace while directing the beat for both **C** and ₵ , cut time halves the actual duration of all notes and rests. This results in a tempo that's twice as fast as common time. Thus, in spite of its longer note values, music in cut time can move rather quickly.

Duet No. 13b is Duet No. 13a in cut time. The quicker tempo gives it a pleasing lilt not possible at a slower tempo.

Duet No. 13b

Humming Song II

S–H

Duet No. 14

Dialogue

A. H.

Solo No. 5 requires you to skip from ② to ④. This downward skip with p is a bit more challenging than the upward skip — after sounding ②, you must suddenly change direction and skip over ③ to reach ④.

Dance of the Downward Skip

Practice Solos 4 and 5 in common time until you can play them fluently. Then practice them in cut time. Never try to play faster than you can accurately direct the beat and solfege. If you make errors, review your Pre-Reading Procedure. Practice slowly and carefully, use the metronome, and check your technique often.

E (Mi), F (Fa), and G (So) on ①

Since you'll use the rest-stroke to play notes on ①, before you begin, thoroughly study "Training the Right-Hand Fingers" in *Part One,* pp. 49 – 53.

As with D at III on ②, if you can't comfortably reach G at III with 3, use 4.

Practice Duet No. 15 with i only, then m, then a. Use prepared rest-strokes. Also, play as slowly as you need for accuracy and confidence, even though the time signature is 𝄵 .

Mi-Fa-So

Duet No. 15

A. H.

Duet No. 16 consists of notes on the first and second strings. This means that you must begin to consider the ease and convenience of right-hand fingering. M, the longer finger, more easily reaches the higher string,①; i, the shorter finger, more easily reaches the lower string,②. Thus, to minimize tension and improve your rest-stroke security, sound ① with m and sound ② with i.

For now, immediately after sounding a string with rest-stroke, each finger should remain against its lower adjacent string until the other finger contacts its string. (An exception occurs, of course, when you must sound the lower adjacent string immediately after sounding the higher string.)

Stepping Tones

Duet No. 16

A. H.

When you feel secure with i and m, practice Duet No. 16 with m and a.

Playing Scale Passages Involving ③, ②, and ①

Playing notes on two adjacent strings presents few problems — you use m on the higher string and i on the lower string, and your right hand never changes position. Passages involving three strings, however, require special consideration.

For example, observe the following scale passage:

Ex. 18

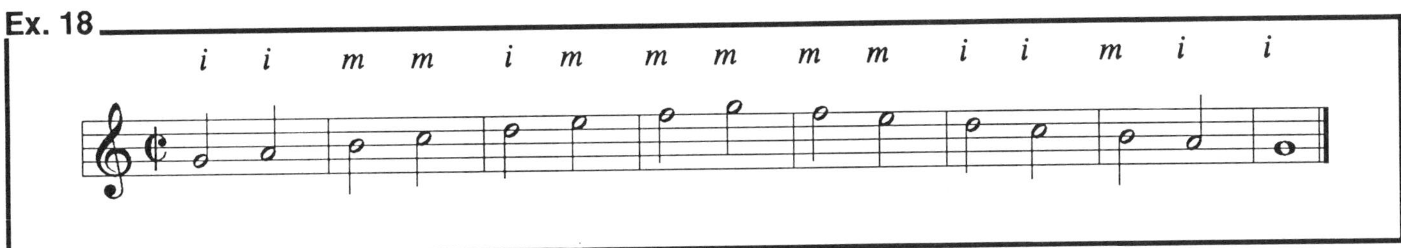

There are two right-hand shifts: one between the second and third measures, and one between the sixth and seventh measures. In the upward shift, you must lower your hand and forearm the distance of one string — i then sounds D (Re) on ②, and m sounds E (Mi) on ①. In the downward shift, you must raise your hand and forearm the distance of one string — m then sounds B (Ti) on ②, and i sounds A (La) on ③.

As Ex. 18 illustrates, you shouldn't use the same finger to sound consecutive notes on adjacent strings. For accuracy and ease, you should use m to reach the higher string and i to reach the lower string.

Chimes

Duet No. 17

A.H.

The Open Fifth and Sixth Strings

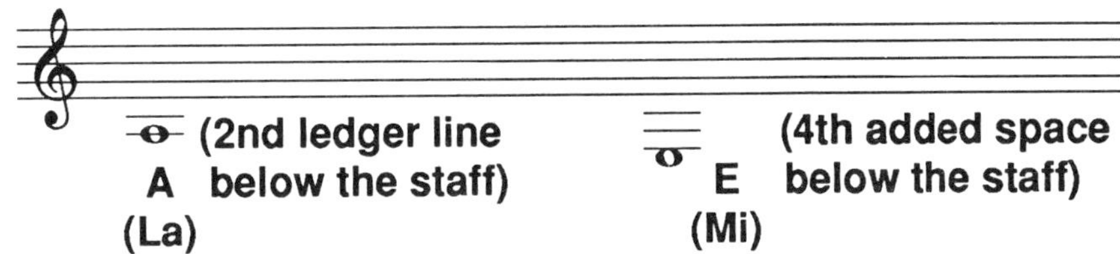

Using p, practice the following examples. Carefully observe the rhythms, and solfege the notes as you play. To stabilize your hand, place the tips of i and m on ② and ③.

Ex. 19a

Ex. 19b (A Rhythmic Variation of 19a)

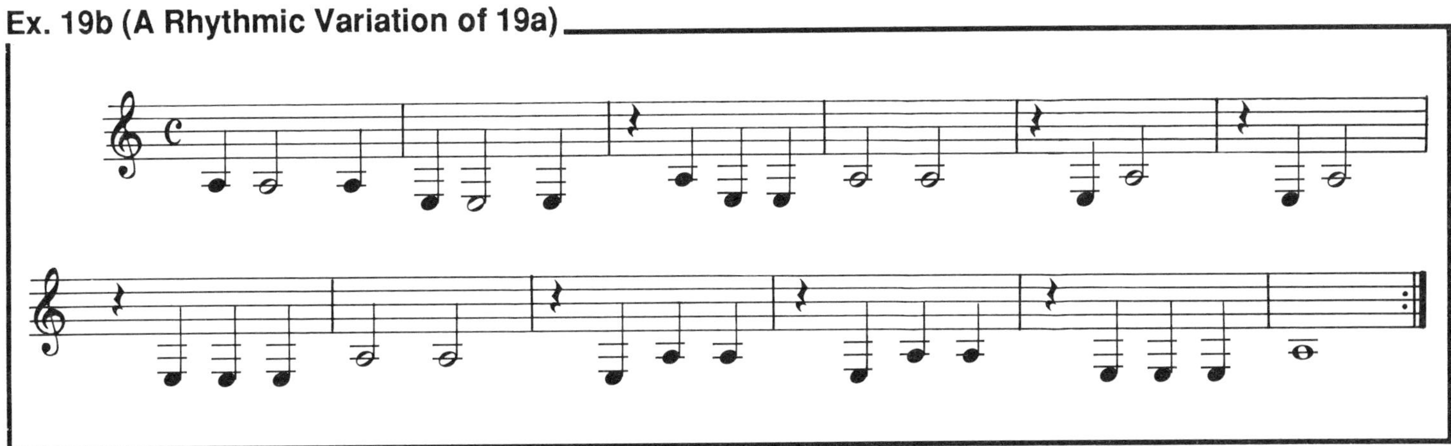

Ex. 20 and Duet No. 18 give you further practice in the downward skip with p sounding ④, then skipping over ⑤ to sound ⑥. Practice Ex. 20 carefully. As before, watch your right hand to ensure the accurate placement of p. Then look away and continue practicing until you can execute this movement form accurately and confidently.

Ex. 20

March

Duet No. 18

S-H

The Tie

The *tie* is a curved line joining two notes of the same pitch. Each of the two notes may be of any time value. When joined by a tie, these notes are sounded as one note equal in duration to the value of both. Tied notes are counted the same as untied notes.

The tie is commonly used in two ways:

1. It indicates that a pitch must be sustained over the bar line.

Ex. 21a

Ex. 21b

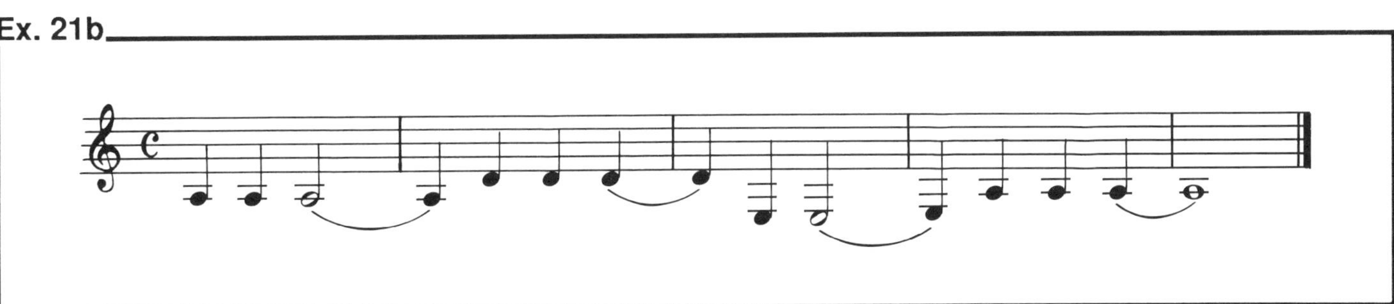

2. It makes rhythmic figures easier to read. For example, although both of the following rhythmic figures are identical, the upper notation is easier to read.

Ex. 22

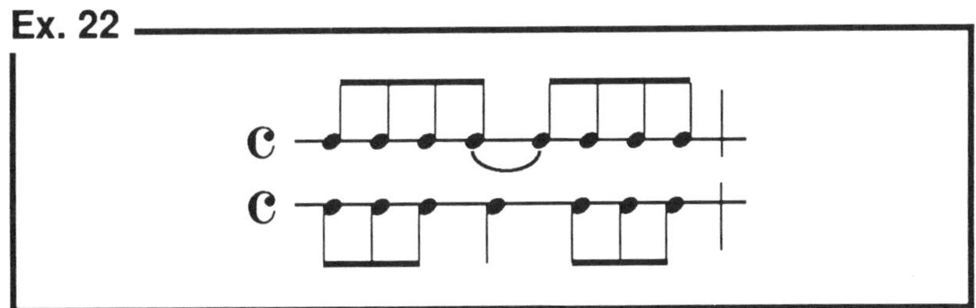

Solo Playing of Music in Two Parts

Solo No. 6 consists of two parts — a treble melody and a bass accompaniment. The piece is notated in a manner commonly used for guitar music: note stems which point upward indicate the melody, and note stems which point downward indicate the rhythmic pattern of the bass. This makes the rhythm of the two parts surprisingly easy to read.

The entire piece is counted "1 & 2 & 3 & 4 &." Notice that the melody notes are sounded on either 1, 2, 3, or 4; thus, each bass note which immediately follows a melody note is sounded on "&."

To avoid confusion and error, carry out the three-step Pre-Reading Procedure before you play the piece. Then practice only the melody until you can play it easily; then play both the melody and bass together.

As you play this piece, you'll find that there will be some overlapping of sound between successive notes, particularly when open strings are involved. For now, make no effort to dampen these sounds. To produce the best possible tone, give careful attention to the firm placement of your fingers and p.

Serenade I

Solo No. 6

A. S.

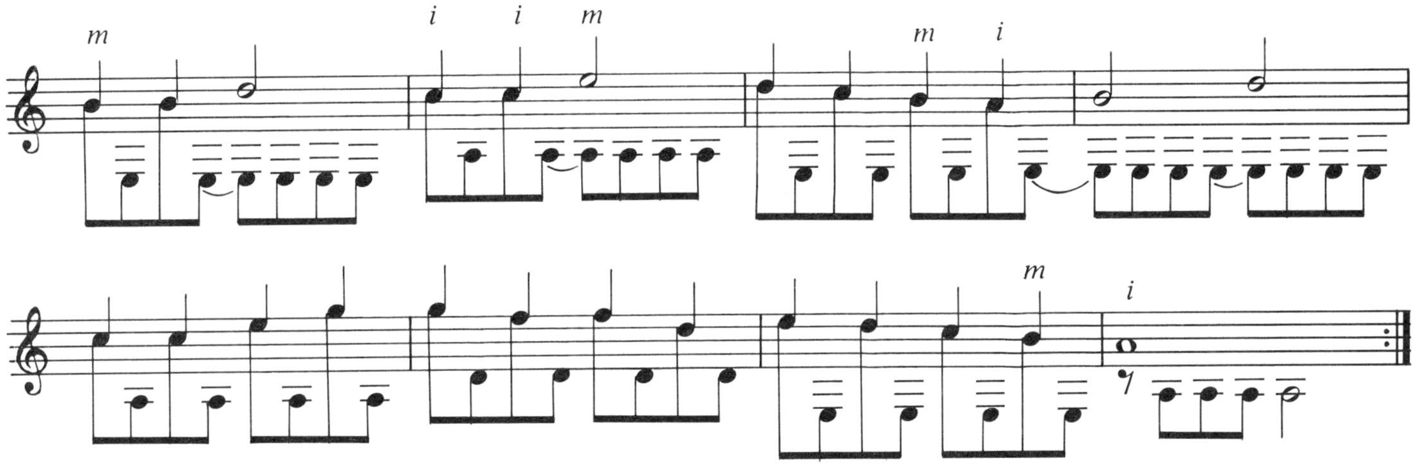

Syncopation

Syncopation occurs when a note with a duration of one beat (or longer) is sounded on the second half (↑ or &) of the beat:

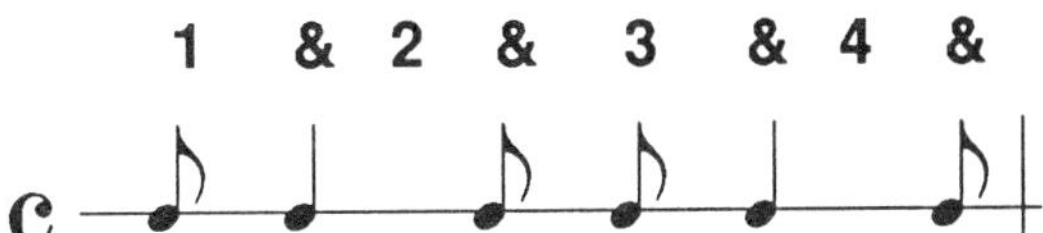

Rhythmic contrast between the melody and bass makes music interesting. If the melody falls on the beat, syncopation of the accompanying bass adds variety. One of the most rewarding aspects of learning to read music on the guitar is the ease with which rhythmic contrasts can be notated and read.

One of the most common syncopated figures is the eighth–quarter–eighth combination: ♪ ♩ ♪ or 𝄾 ♩ ♪ . The down-up method of directing the beat makes this rhythmic figure relatively easy to understand. The quarter note ♩ equals two tied eighth notes ♫ ; when a ♩ occurs on ↑ (or "&"), the next value will occur on the next ↑ (or the next "&").

The following version of Solo No. 6 contains the eighth–quarter–eighth rhythmic variation (R.V.) in the bass. Remember to use the metronome.

Serenade II

Solo No. 6 R. V.

M.M. ♩= 66

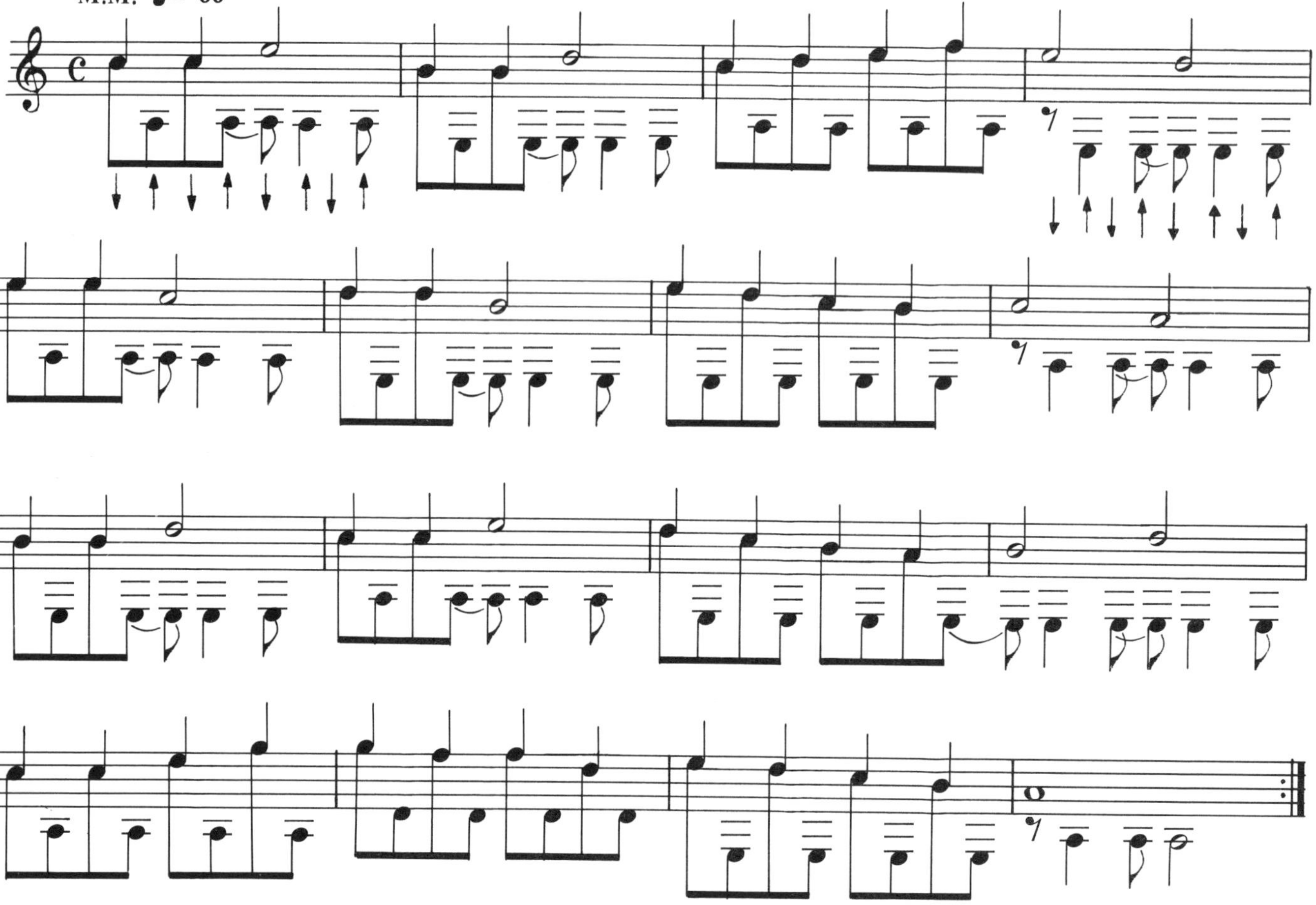

G♯ (Si)† on ③

Specific symbols are used to indicate that a note is to be played either higher or lower in pitch. These symbols are called ***chromatic signs.*** Notes which aren't altered by a chromatic sign are called ***natural.*** The sharp sign, ♯, indicates that a note is to be played a half step (one fret) higher than its natural pitch. The flat sign, ♭, indicates that a note is to be played a half step (one fret) lower than its natural pitch.

Solo No. 7 introduces G♯ on ③—it's located at the 1st fret and is notated as follows:

†All solfege syllables representing notes with a single sharp are pronounced with an "ee" sound. For example, "si" is pronounced "see." For an explanation of solfege syllables and their pronunciations, see "Solfege," p. 209.

Slavic Dance I

Solo No. 7

A. S.

As in Solo No. 6–R.V., the rhythmic variation in Solo No. 7–R.V. is in the bass.

Slavic Dance II

Solo No. 7 R. V.

A. S.

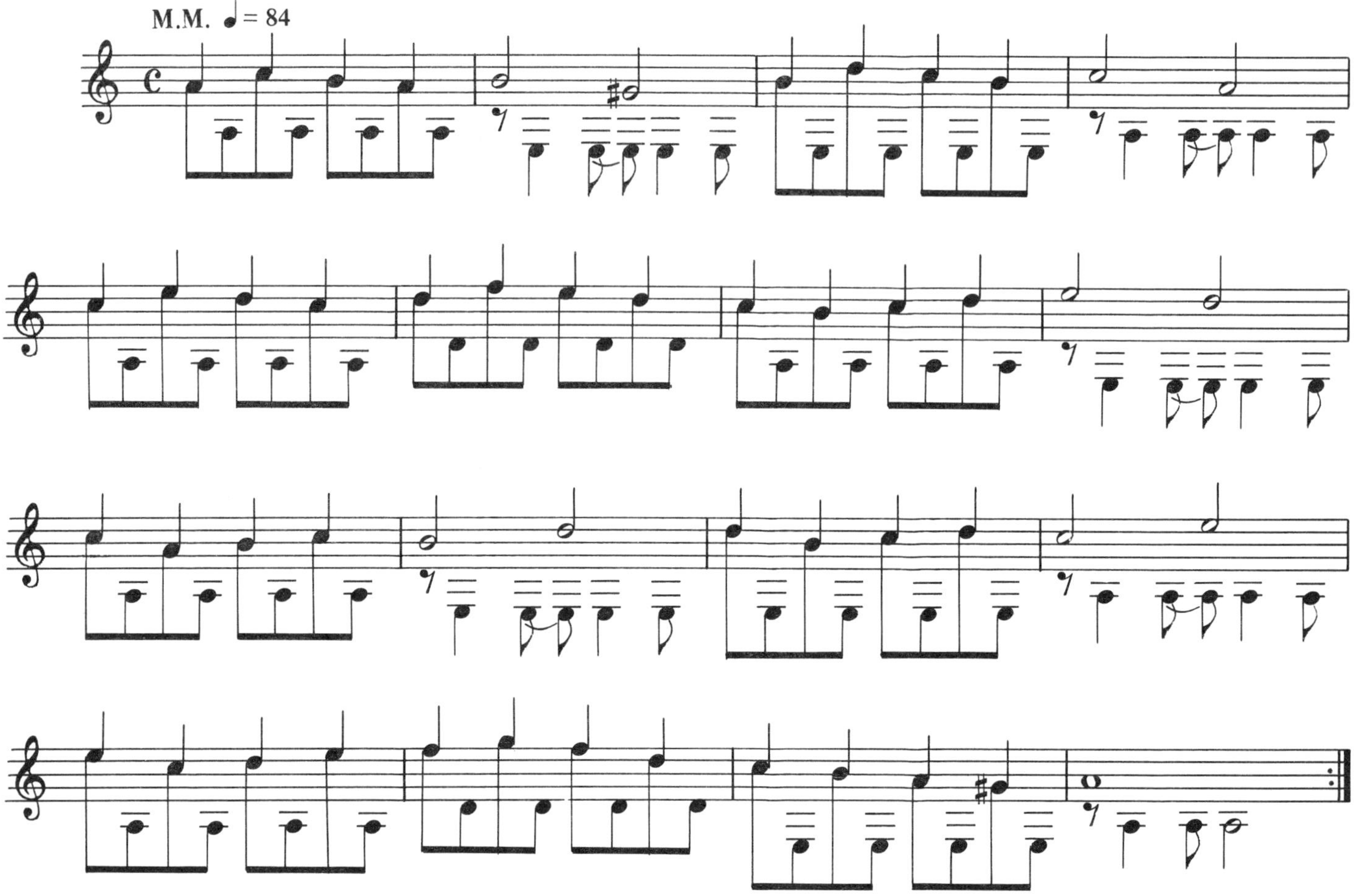

M.M. ♩ = 84

3/4 Time and the Dotted Half Value

A dot placed after a note or rest increases its time value by half that value: 𝅗𝅥. equals 𝅗𝅥‿♩ and 𝄼. equals 𝄼 𝄽

The 3/4 time signature establishes triple meter.

Ex. 23

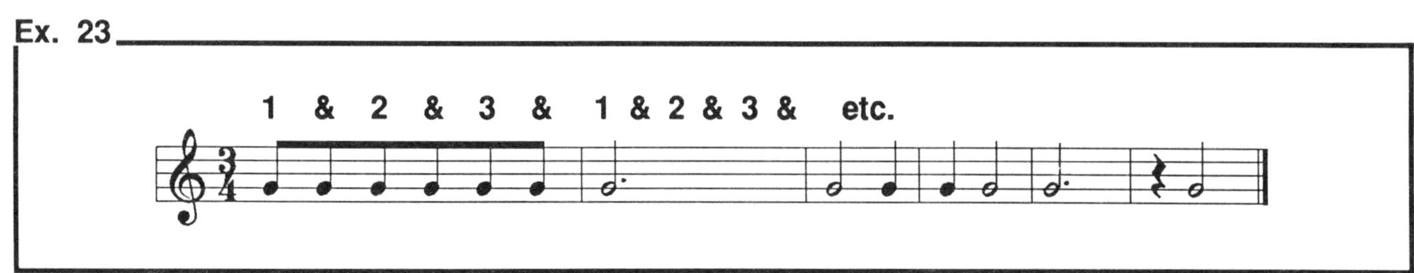

Folk Song

Solo No. 8

A. S.

M.M. ♩= 88

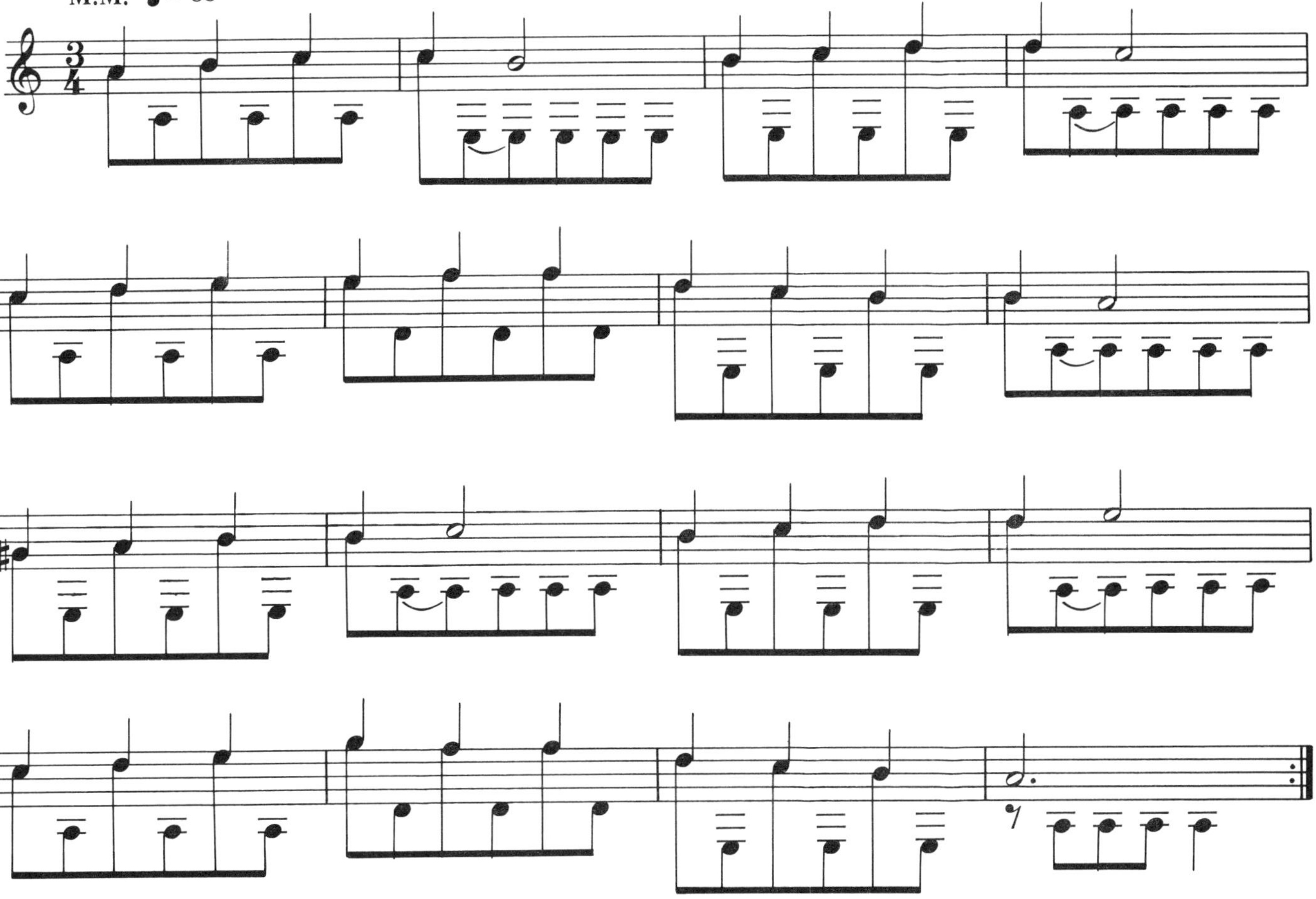

The Dotted Quarter Value

The next element of rhythmic variation to be introduced is the dotted quarter value (♩. or 𝄽.). Since a dot placed after a note or rest increases its time value by half, ♩. = ♩‿♪ , and 𝄽. = 𝄽𝄾

When the time signature indicates that the quarter note represents one beat, you should count and direct the dot as the first half of the next beat — the note or rest following the dot occurs on "&" (↑):

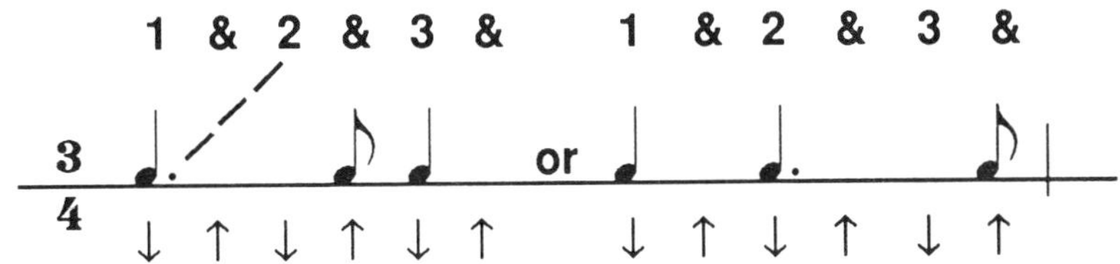

When a dotted quarter note appears in the melody (as in Solo No. 8–R.V.), you can most easily understand and perform it by observing its relationship to the bass.

In Solo No. 8–R.V., you'll use adjacent fingers to sound the ♪♩ which follows the ♩. . Slightly lift the finger with which you've sounded the ♪ while sounding the ♩ with the alternate finger.

Folk Dance

Beginning Free-Stroke: Sounding Two Notes Simultaneously

Before proceeding, carefully review "Beginning Free-Stroke with Your Fingers," *Part One*, pp. 55 – 62.

Assuming you haven't already begun, you'll begin training 4 (the fourth finger of your left hand) in the following examples. In actual or implied chord formations, 4 is often used instead of 3 to form either the note G (So) on ① or D (Re) on ②.

A horizontal dash following the finger number (1-, 2-) indicates that the finger continues to be lightly held down. In Exs. 24 through 26, 1- serves as a secure point of reference for accurately placing 4.

When using two or more left-hand fingers together, be especially careful to keep all three finger joints comfortably flexed, and place each fingertip close to its respective fret. This ensures that you'll get a clear sound with a minimum of left-hand tension.†

In the following example, there are three different pairs of notes — you should identify them by solfeging each note and naming each left-hand finger. Repeat until you can clearly see in your mind's eye the location and left-hand formation of each pair of notes on the fingerboard. Before playing, you should be able to read and visualize the complete example (solfeging the top note of each note pair) at a slow and steady tempo. Then carefully play the example, solfeging the top note as you play.

Ex. 24

†See *Part One*, pp. 44 – 45.

Proceed in a similar manner with the following examples:

Ex. 25

Ex. 26

Two by Two

Duet No. 19

A. H.

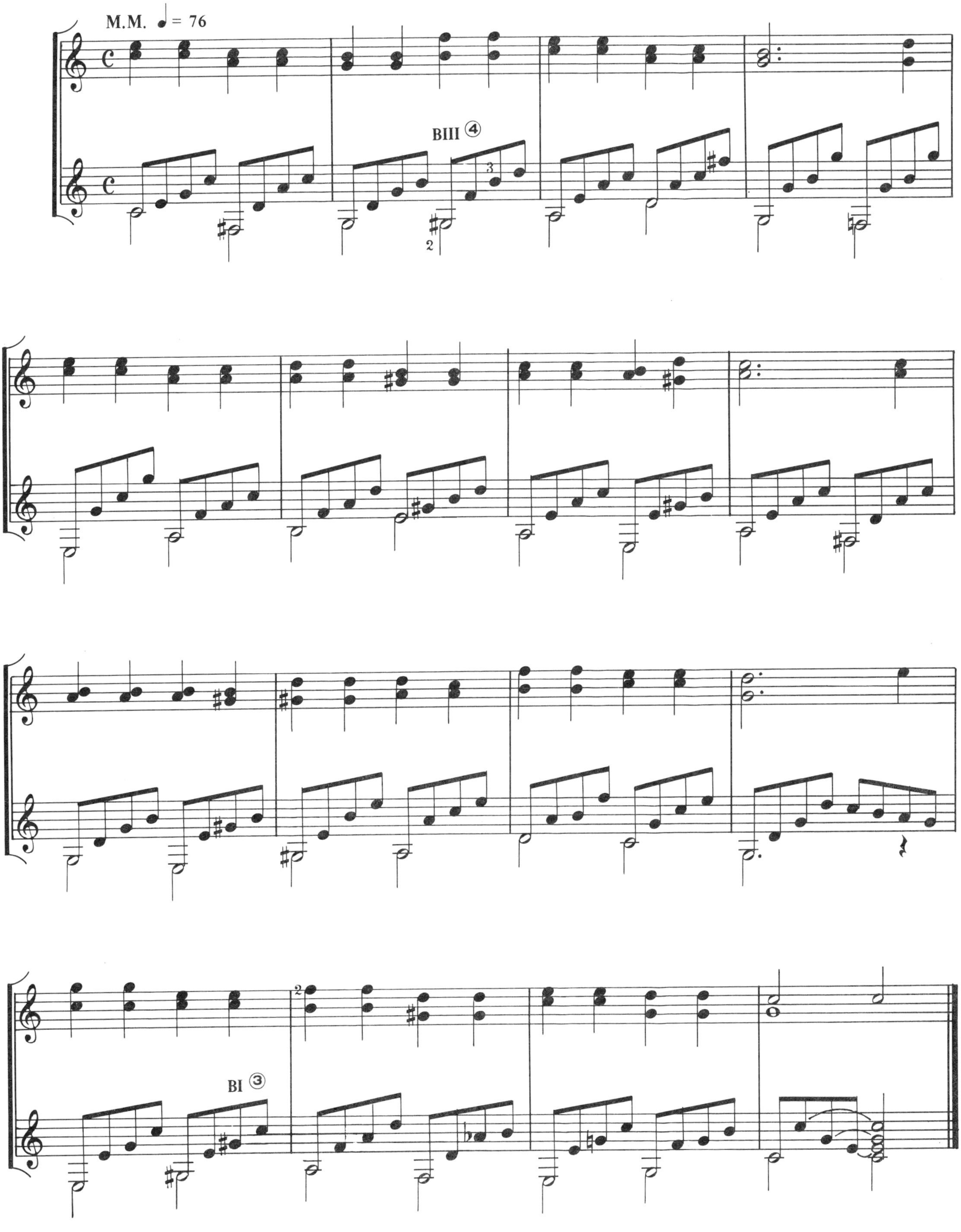

M.M. ♩ = 76

BIII ④

3

2

BI ③

2

Petite Valse

Duet No. 20

A. H.

m m
1.
2.
BV ③

F♯ (Fi) on ① and C♯ (Di) on ②

F♯ (Fi) and C♯ (Di) are located on II. They're notated as follows:

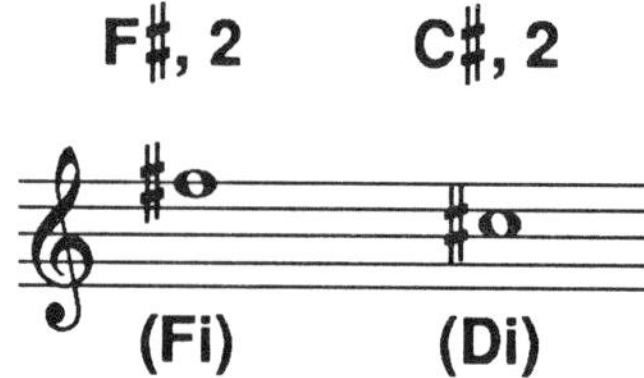

The Key Signature

When a chromatically altered note appears repeatedly throughout a piece, placing the chromatic sign before each note is often avoided by placing the sign on the appropriate line or space of the staff just after the clef. For example, indicates that all the notes F and C are to be sharped throughout the piece. Chromatic signs placed in this manner are called the ***key signature.***[†]

The consecutive use of 2 and 3 is introduced in the following examples. Be sure to place each finger close to its fret, and lightly hold each finger down until the formation of another note demands that the finger be lifted.

After thoroughly carrying out the Pre-Reading Procedure, practice the following examples (rest-stroke) until fluent.

Ex. 27

Ex. 28

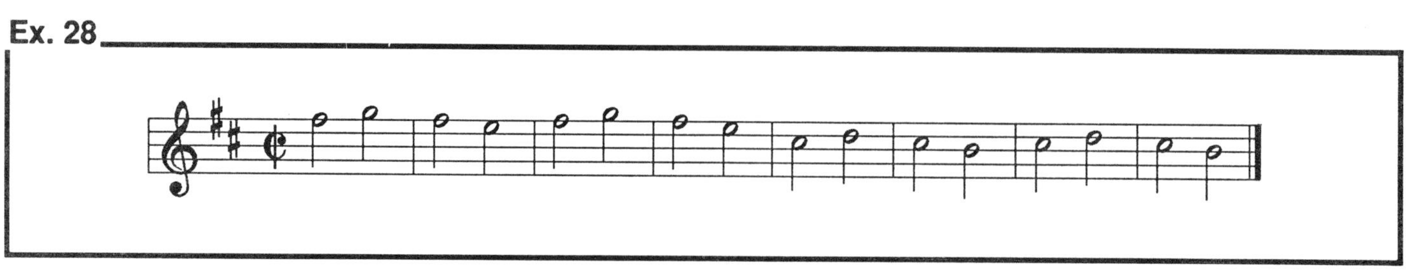

[†]A thorough understanding of keys, key signatures, and other elements of music is essential for learning to play the guitar well. See my *Basic Elements of Music Theory for the Guitar*, CPP-Belwin, 15800 N.W. 48th Ave., Miami, FL 33014.

Ex. 29

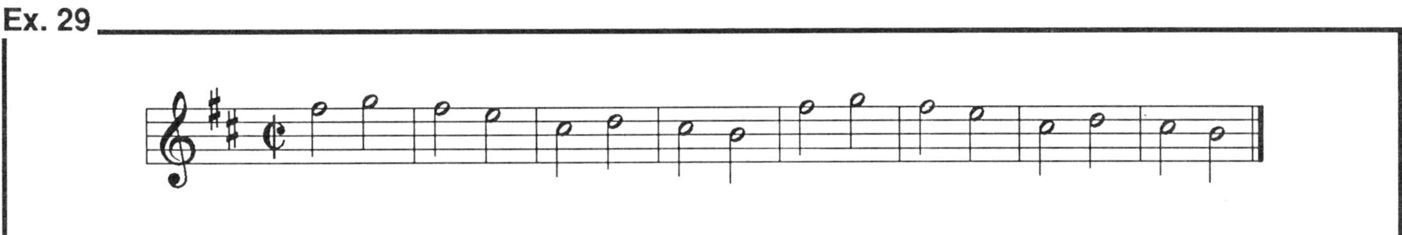

Ex. 30

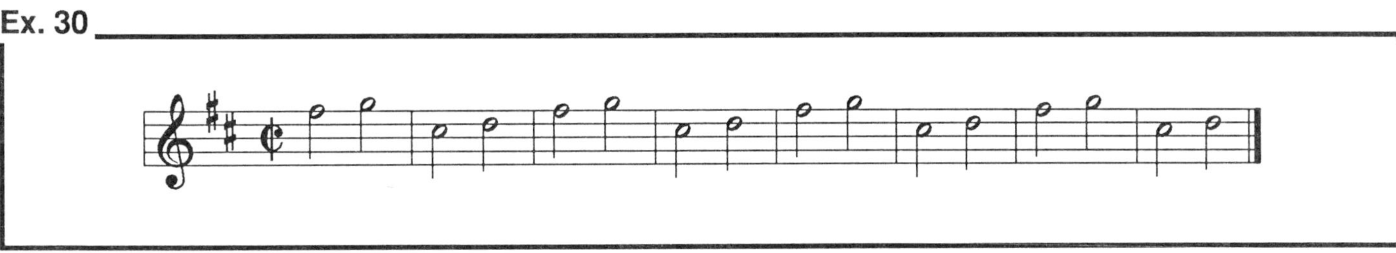

Ex. 31

Andante I

Solo No. 9

A. S.

Andante II

Solo No. 9 R. V.

A. S.

NOTE: Although you'll be shifting your attention between the rest-stroke and free-stroke throughout this book, don't neglect either stroke in your daily practice. When practicing new material in which one stroke is required, be sure to include a review of past material using the other stroke. Since you need to be proficient with both rest-stroke and free-stroke to play the guitar well, you should maintain a balanced development of both.

Further Training of the Fourth Finger

You'll now proceed with the next step in training 4: forming successive notes with 4 and 3 (or 3 and 4) moving consecutively. Because of the lack of independence between these fingers, you need to approach the training of 3 and 4 with special care. You'll begin with one of the easiest consecutive movements of 3 and 4: forming notes on adjacent strings at the same fret:

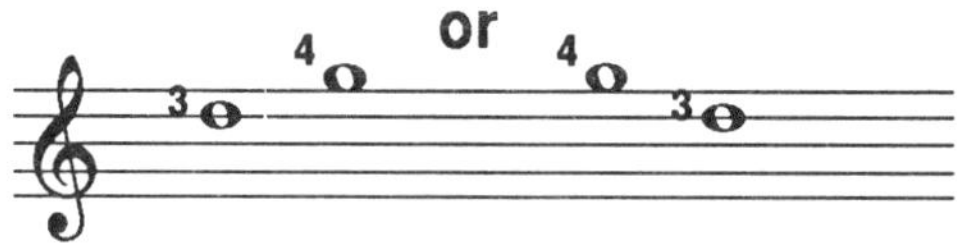

As you approach Exs. 32 and 33, be sure to observe the following:

> **• Hold your left elbow somewhat sideways from your body.**
>
> **• Slightly rotate your forearm so that the right side of your palm (near the fourth finger) is away from the edge of the fingerboard.**
>
> **• Be sure to place each finger close to its fret; after sounding the note, lightly hold each finger down until the formation of another note demands that the finger be lifted.**

Don't neglect to solfege and visualize the examples before you play. You can further clarify the examples by naming the left-hand fingerings as you direct the beat. If you can't do these preparatory steps without hesitation at a reasonable tempo, you're not adequately prepared to play. *For rapid and secure progress, it's essential that you thoroughly understand each exercise before you begin to play.*

Individually practice each figure in Exs. 32 and 33 until you can easily play them all. Then practice the figures in unbroken succession.

Ex. 32

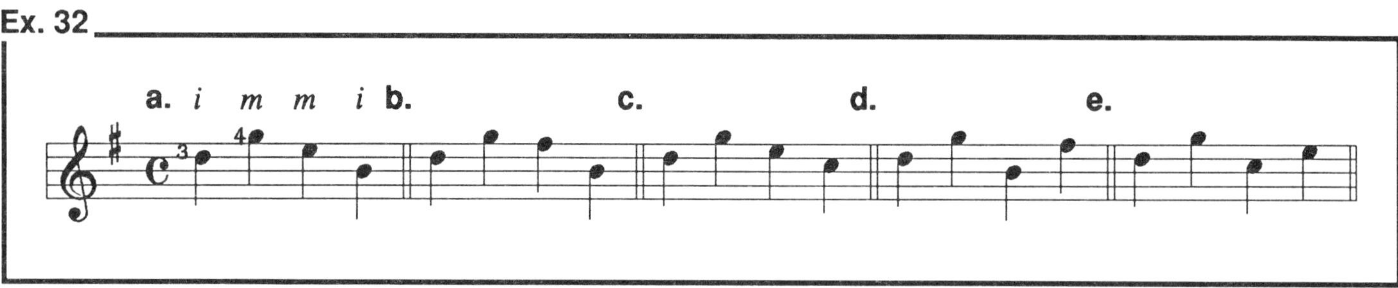

Ex. 33

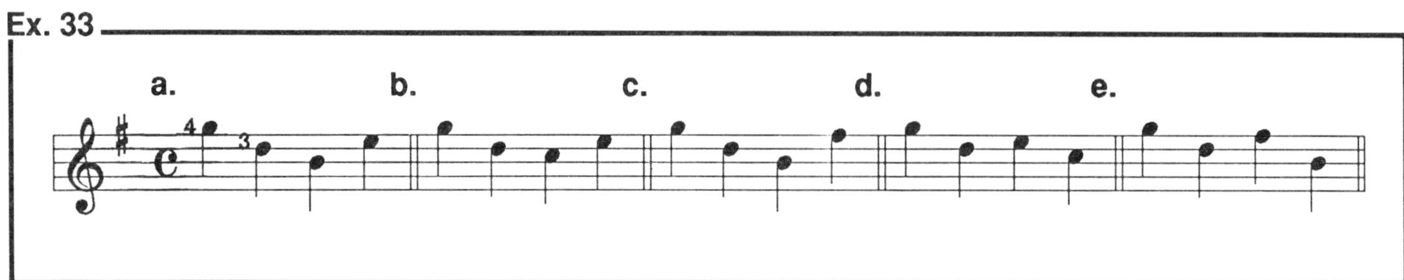

Accidentals in Music

Any chromatic sign which appears in a piece but not in the key signature is called an ***accidental.*** For example, the G♯ introduced in Solo No. 7 (see p. 47) is an accidental. C♯ appears in Duet No. 21, but only F♯ is found in the key signature — thus, C♯ is an accidental. *An accidental is effective only for the remainder of the measure in which it appears.*

To cancel an accidental, the ***natural sign*** ♮ is used. The natural sign can also be used to cancel out a chromatic sign which appears in the key signature — when used in this manner, the natural sign is considered an accidental. *Whether canceling an accidental or canceling a chromatic sign which appears in the key signature, a natural sign is effective only for the remainder of the measure in which it appears.*

Although an accidental is effective only for the remainder of the measure in which it appears, performers sometimes forget to cancel it in the measures which follow. To remind the musician to cancel an accidental, composers and publishers sometimes insert a chromatic sign in a following measure. To distinguish it from an accidental, modern editions often place this chromatic sign in parentheses. For example, in measures 10 and 21 of Duet 21, you'll find a natural sign in parentheses (♮) — this reminds you that the C♯ in measures 7 and 19 is no longer effective.

Duet No. 21

Carillon

S - H

M.M. ♩= 112

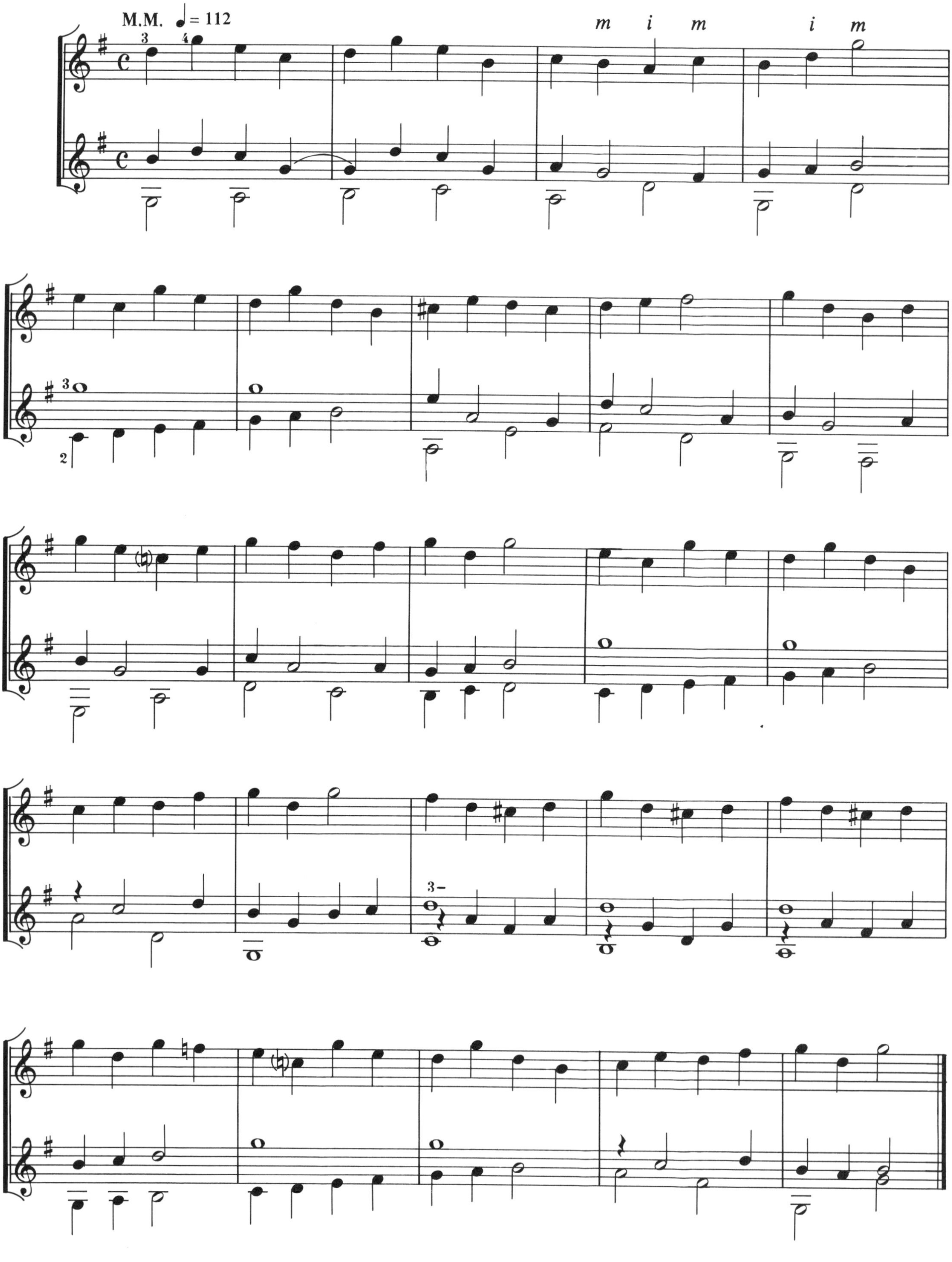

m i m i m

Carefully observe the accidentals C♯ and F♮ in Solo No. 10 during your Pre-Reading Procedure, and also become thoroughly familiar with all fingerings. Although the fingering isn't difficult, changing accurately from one formation to the next requires considerable practice and clear aim-directed movement.[†]

Also notice the double bar ‖ in measures 16 and 32. Composers occasionally use this to indicate the end of a musical period or section. In Solo No. 10, a double bar marks the end of each 16-measure period.

Longer reaches with p to the low bass strings are purposely avoided in Solo No. 10. Thus, you can more easily keep the middle joints of your right-hand fingers well flexed while minimizing tension in p, and you can also concentrate on the quality of your tone.

[†]For an explanation of aim-directed movement, see *Part One,* pp. 4 – 5.

Solo No. 10

Music Box I

S-H

M.M. ♩= 84

Music Box II

S - H

Solos 11 and 11–R.V. provide further practice in alternating a finger rest-stroke with p free-stroke.

Cantilena I

Solo No. 11

A. S.

Cantilena II

Solo No. 11 R. V.

A. S.

M.M. ♩ = 84

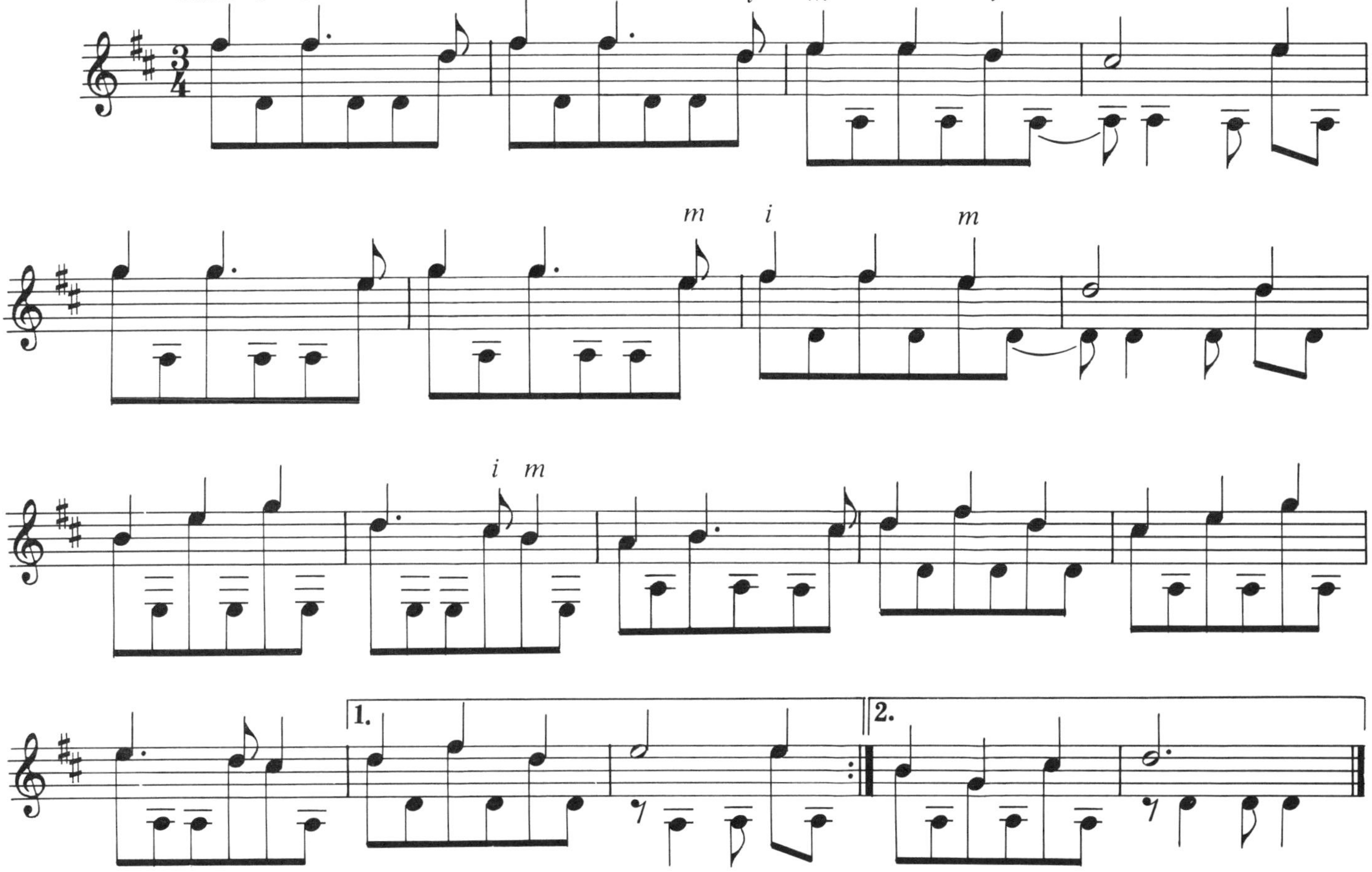

E (Mi) and F (Fa) on ④

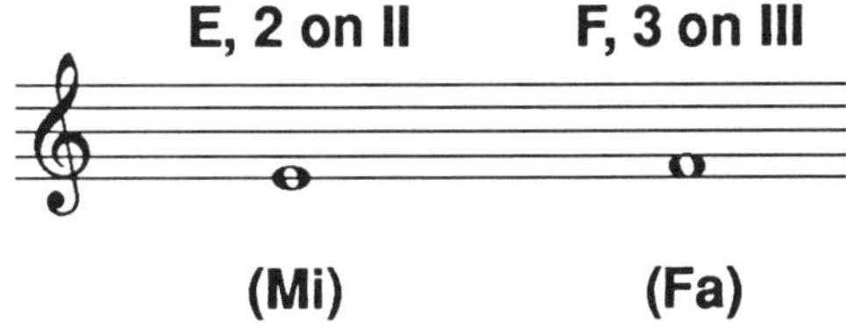

Ex. 34 (with P)

Before playing Solo No. 12, you should become thoroughly familiar with its two chord formations. One chord formation appears for the first time in measure 2, the other in measure 4. You should clearly visualize and practice each formation before playing the piece.

Moorish Dance

Solo No. 12

A. S.

Beginning A Free-Stroke: Chords of Three Notes

Ex. 35a introduces i–m–a sounding a triad of three notes. Be sure to position a advantageously for bringing out the highest note of each triad (see *Part One*, pp. 61 – 62).

Ex. 35a

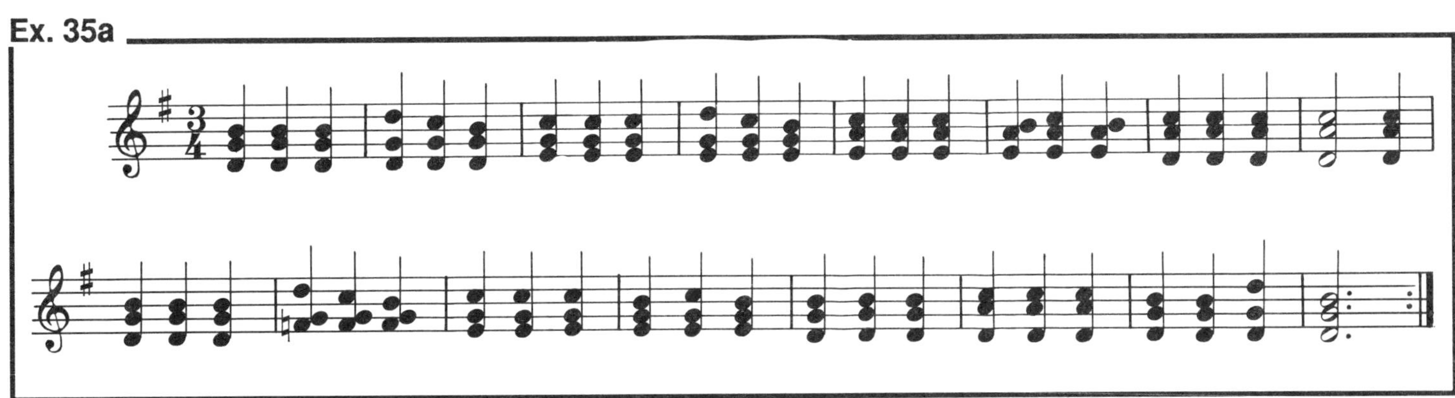

Ex. 35b

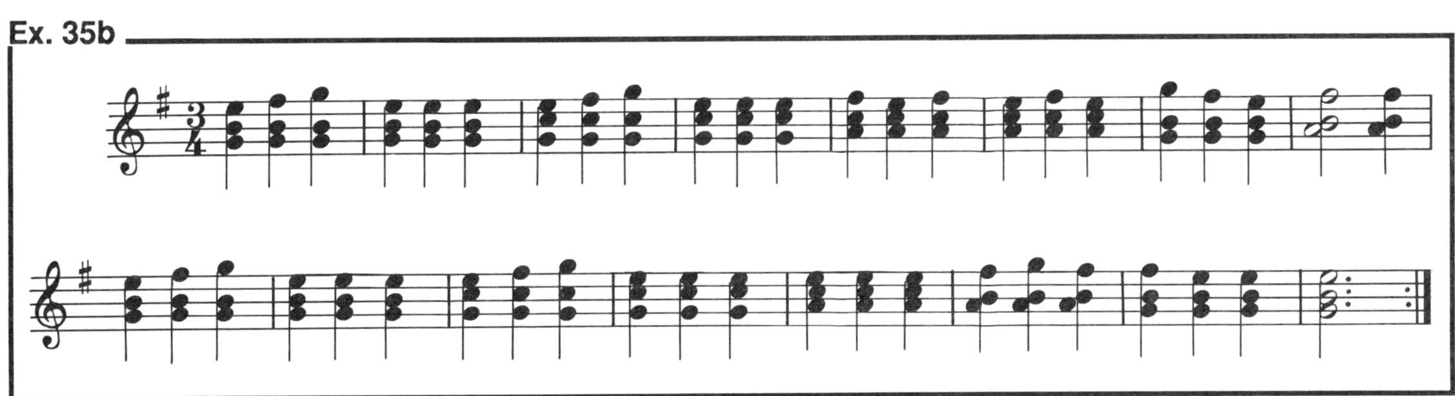

Ex. 36 introduces i–m–a and p alternation. Keep your right hand steady, and maintain the advantageous position of a.

Ex. 36

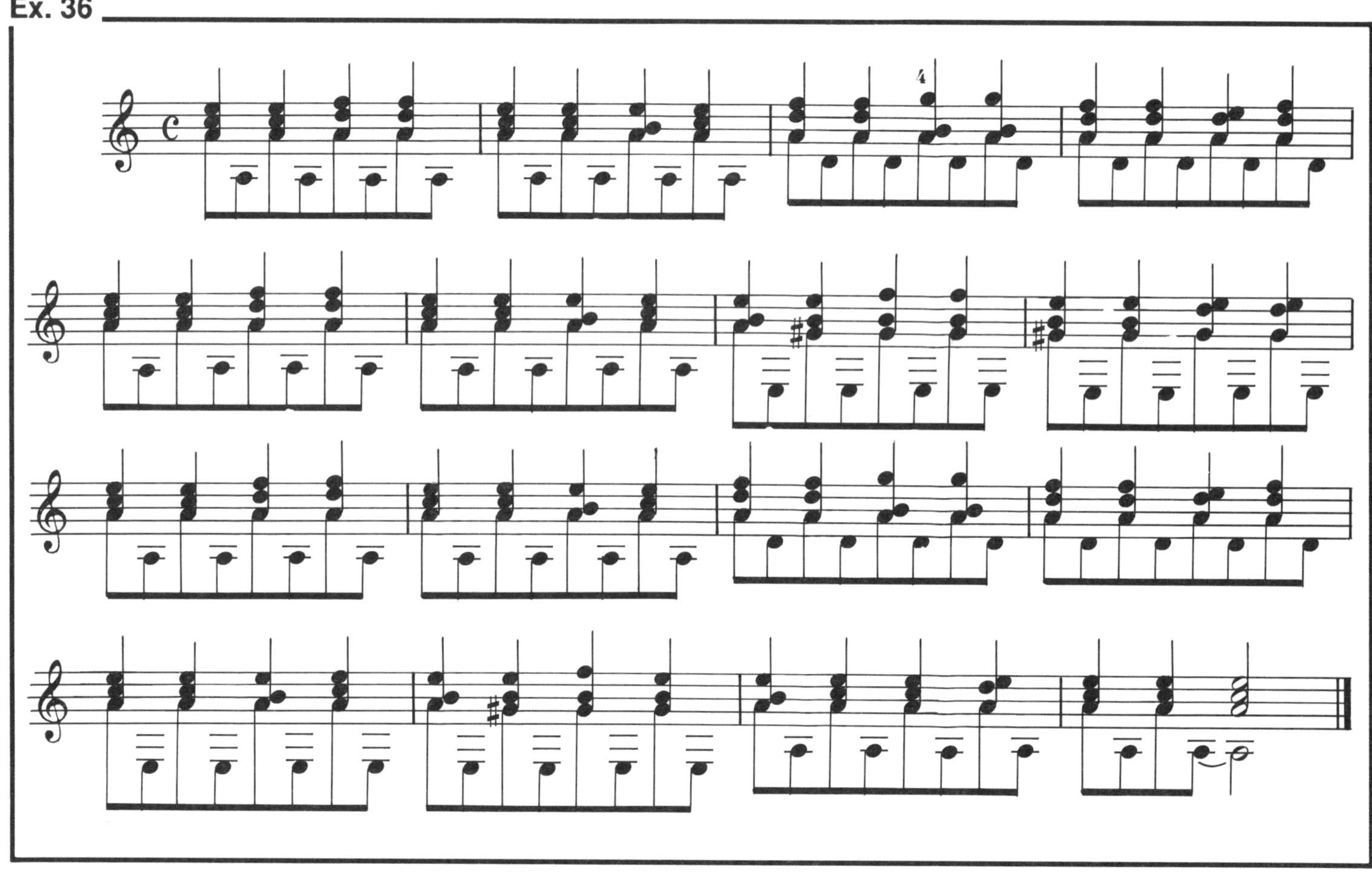

Beginning Arpeggios: Sympathetic Movement

An *arpeggio* consists of the notes of a chord played in succession. You'll begin by focusing on the sympathetic movement within p, i, m (see *Part One*, pp. 63–65). Practice Ex. 37a until you can securely execute it at M.M. ♩ = 150.

Ex. 37a

As you increase the tempo of Ex. 37a, notice that it becomes awkward to direct the beat with three well-defined down-up movements per measure. Thus, you're now ready to learn both a time signature and a manner of directing the beat which are better suited to fast tempos.

Single-Beat Measures of Three Counts

In notating music which moves at a relatively fast tempo, composers often use the 3/8 time signature rather than 3/4. At a rapid tempo, it's easier to direct 3/8 with one down-up movement per measure. Since there's no even division of three notes, the precise timing of the upbeat (↑) is no longer significant. Thus, you should continue to precisely time the downbeat (↓), and execute the upbeat wherever it feels comfortable—approximately between the second and third beats.

When 3/8 is directed in this manner, notice that the beat is now represented by the dotted quarter value:

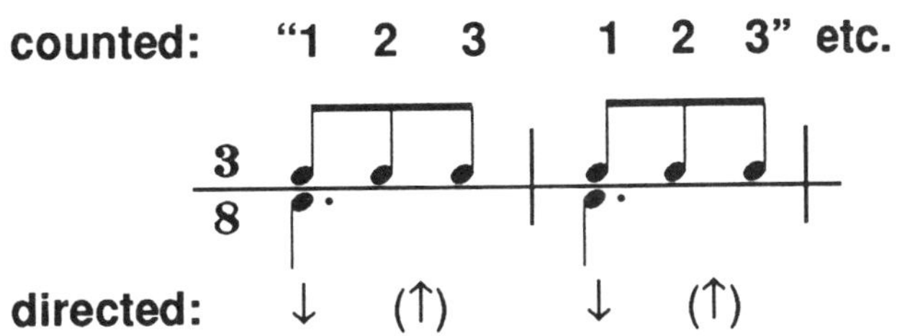

Thus, at rapid tempos, the 3/8 time signature doesn't accurately convey the number of beats per measure.†

Practice this method of counting and directing the beat until you can comfortably carry it out at M.M. ♩. = 50.

Ex. 37b

Carefully observe the key signature of Duet No. 22, and note the two accidentals, G♯ and C♮. Remember, an accidental is effective only for the remainder of the measure in which it appears. Also notice that, between measures 12 and 13, 1 on G♯ (Si) is gently glided along ③ (notated ⁄1) to the 2nd fret to form A (La).

Observe the term "rit." in measure 16. This is an abbreviation of ***ritardando*** (Italian, pronounced "ree-tar-**dahn**-do"), which means "growing slower." Also observe the ***a tempo*** (Italian, pronounced "ah **tem**-po") in measure 17. This indicates a return to the original tempo.

Remember, avoid confusion and error from the beginning of practice. Carefully carry out the Pre-Reading Procedure before you begin playing.

---

†You'll encounter other meters where the time signature doesn't accurately convey the number of beats per measure (see "Compound Meter," p. 104).

The Gondolier

Duet No. 22

A. H.

M.M. ♩. = 50+

By including some movement within the harmony, Duet No. 22 becomes an attractive and contemporary-sounding solo. Observe the natural sign in measure 16 (the natural signs in measures 22 and 25 are simply reminders to cancel out the accidentals in measures 19 and 23).

Carefully observe the B♭ (Te) found on ③ at III. Since III on ③ is one fret above A, it can also be identified as A♯ (Li). Thus, one pitch can be notated two different ways and have two different names. Two notes which are written differently but indicate the same pitch are ***enharmonic.*** B♭ and A♯ are enharmonic notes. The decision about which notation to use is generally based on either harmonic considerations or clarity of writing and reading.

Since at measures 1 and 2 you must hold 2 on F♯ (Fi) on ①, you'll find the reach to C♯ (Di) on ② with 1 is easier when you slightly rotate your forearm clockwise.

Etude Moderne

Solo No. 13

S-H

Further Training of A

Ex. 38a introduces the p, i, m–a movement form (see *Part One*, p. 65). Before you begin, carefully practice the following figure until you can accurately play it at a reasonable tempo:

Ex. 38a

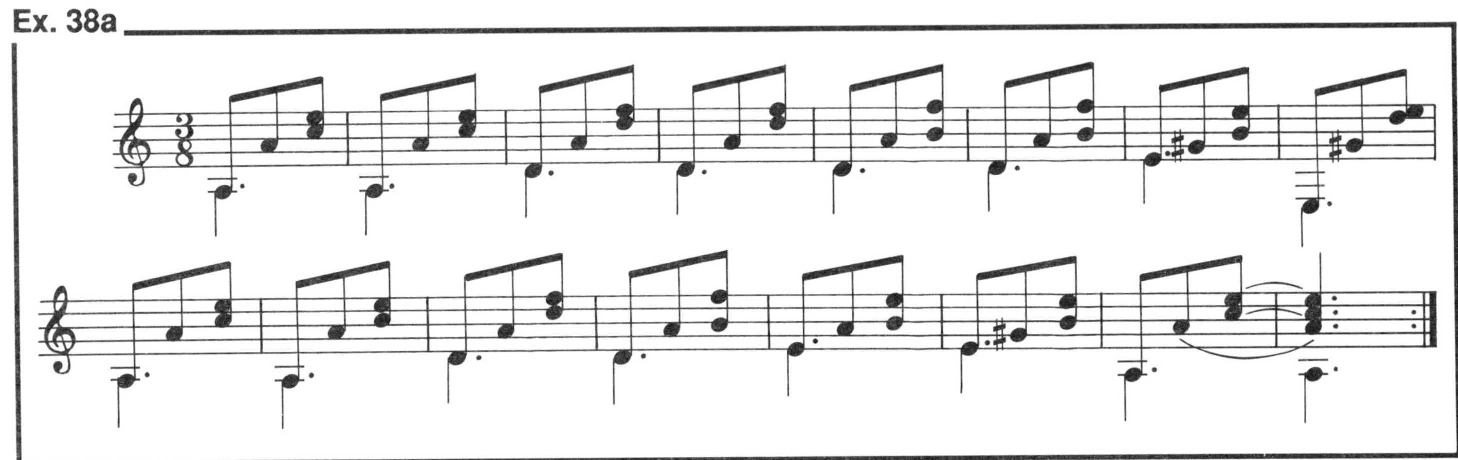

Ex. 38b introduces the p, i–m, a movement form (see *Part One*, p. 66). Again, before you begin the exercise, carefully practice the following figure until you can accurately play it at a reasonable tempo:

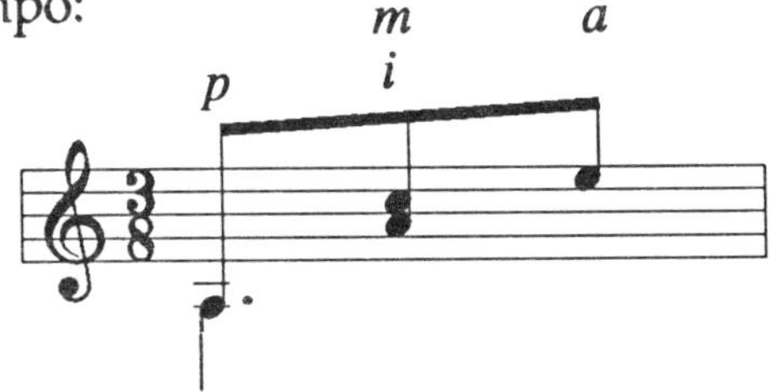

Ex. 38b

Right-Hand Finger Alternation

You'll now begin one of the most demanding aspects of right-hand finger training: acquiring the ability to sound strings accurately, powerfully, and rapidly through successive alternation of two adjacent fingers.

The following exercises and pieces will be rewarding to the extent that you understand how your fingers should move. You'll find information concerning right-hand finger alternation in *Part One*, pp. 67 – 69.

Producing an appealing, powerful, and full-bodied free-stroke tone while fluently alternating the fingers is among the most important requirements for becoming a competent guitarist. Thus, you should also review "Principles of Tone Production," *Part One*, pp. 21 – 28.

You'll begin alternation by playing the p, i, m, i arpeggio. P, i, m, i contains one opposed movement followed by one sympathetic movement:

> **• As m flexes to sound its string, i extends to prepare on its string — this is the opposed (alternation) movement.**
>
> **• As m follows through, i flexes to sound its string — this is the sympathetic movement.**

Carefully practice this arpeggio until you can execute it with reasonable fluency:

Avoid the tendency to rush the process of learning to play. Your patience and careful practice will be rewarded with secure accomplishment.

The Sixteenth Value

The sixteenth note, 𝅘𝅥𝅯 or 𝅘𝅥𝅯, and the sixteenth rest, 𝄿, each equal one-half the value of one eighth note or rest. Thus, two sixteenth notes, ♬, or two sixteenth rests, 𝄿 𝄿, equal one eighth value.

Solo No. 14 introduces the 4/8 time signature. In 4/8, the eighth value now represents one beat. Counting, however, should cause no difficulty. You should direct the beat in a manner similar to 4/4 — the eighth value replaces the quarter value, and the sixteenth value replaces the eighth value.

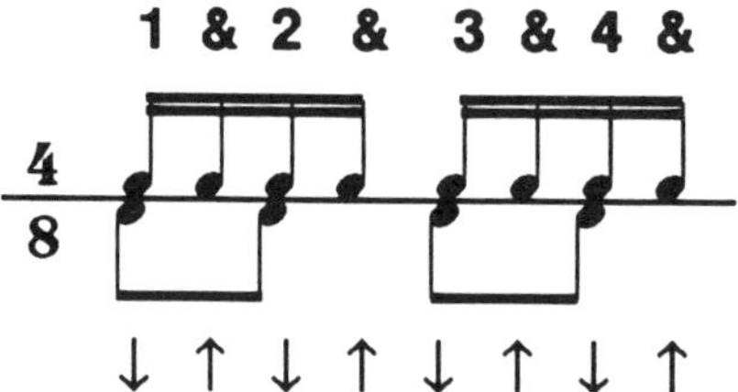

As indicated above, groups of sixteenth notes are commonly beamed together.

In addition to providing right-hand training, Solo No. 14 also includes further training for the left-hand third and fourth fingers. Previous material has required you to place the fourth finger at III on ①, preceded or followed by placing the third finger at III on ②. Several measures of Solo No. 14 require you to place the third and fourth fingers on ④ and ② respectively — both at III. Thus, the two fingers will be separated by one string.

Remember to visualize the left-hand finger formations of each of the following arpeggio studies. Before playing the entire piece, isolate and practice new formations until you can play them fluently.

P,I,M,I Etude I

A. S.

Solo No. 14

Solo No. 15

P, I, M, I Etude II

A. S.

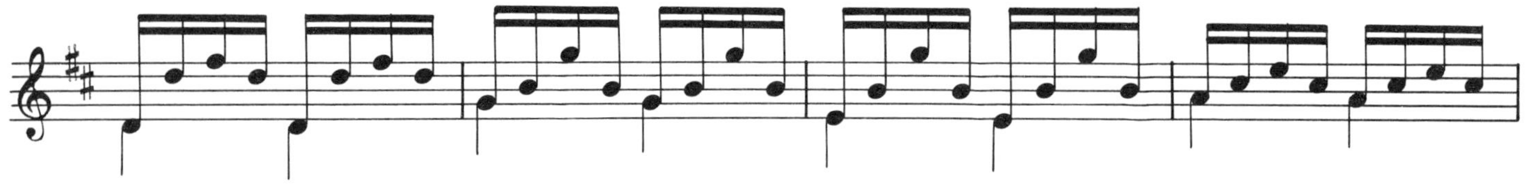

B (Ti) and C (Do) on ⑤

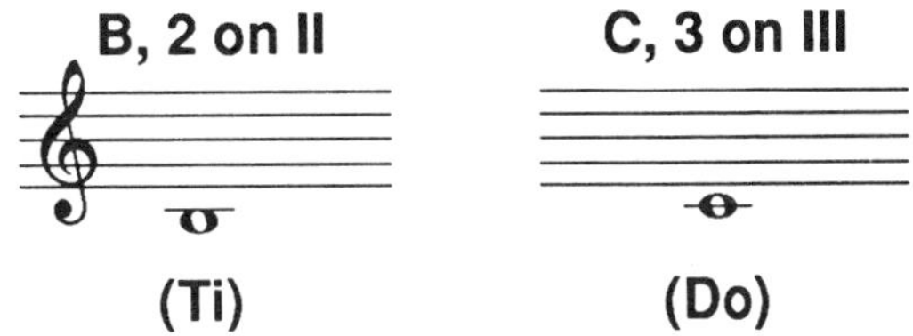

Ex. 39 (P, Free-Stroke)

Duet No. 23

Romance

A.H.

Solo No. 16

P, I, M, I Etude III

S-H

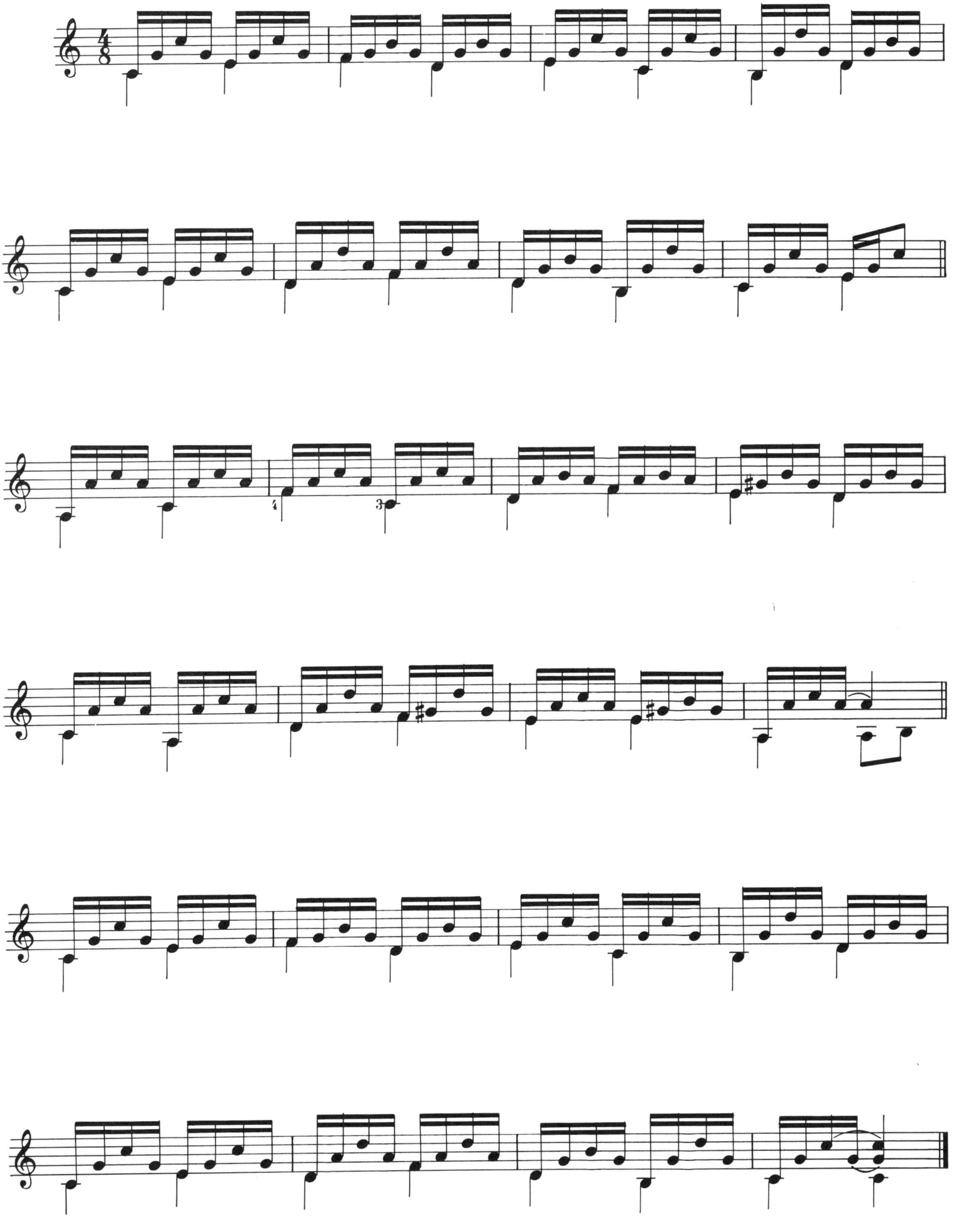

4 3

Arpeggios Requiring Further Alternation

Solo No. 17 is Solo No. 16 rewritten in 3/8. This arpeggio figure requires three alternations, and ends with the sympathetic follow-through of i with m.

Solo No. 17

P, I, M, I, M, I Etude

Exs. 40a and 40b introduce alternation involving a: p, i, m–a, i and p, i–m, a, i–m. (See *Part One*, p. 70.)

Ex. 40a (P, I, M–A, I)

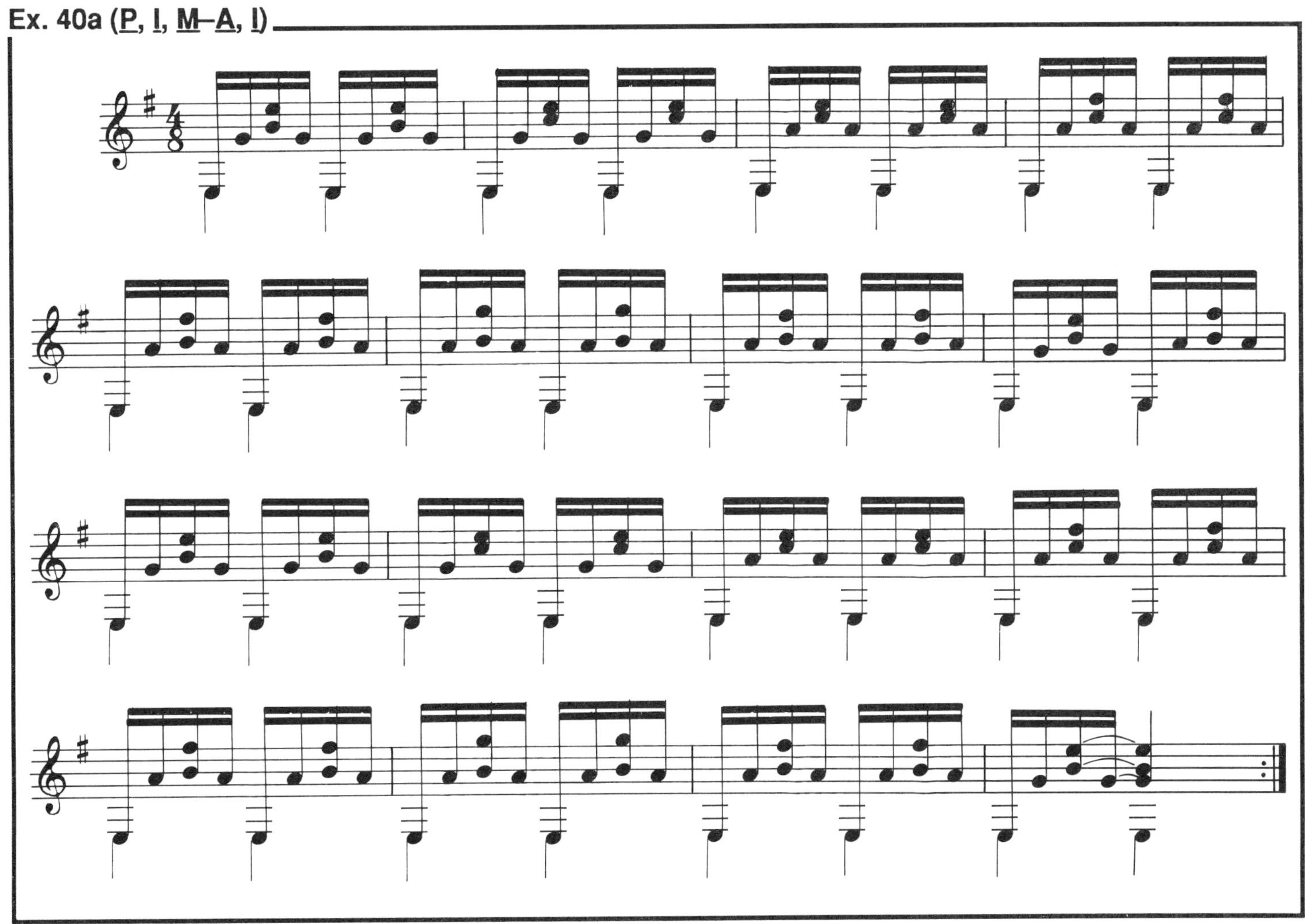

Ex. 40b (P, I–M, A, I–M)

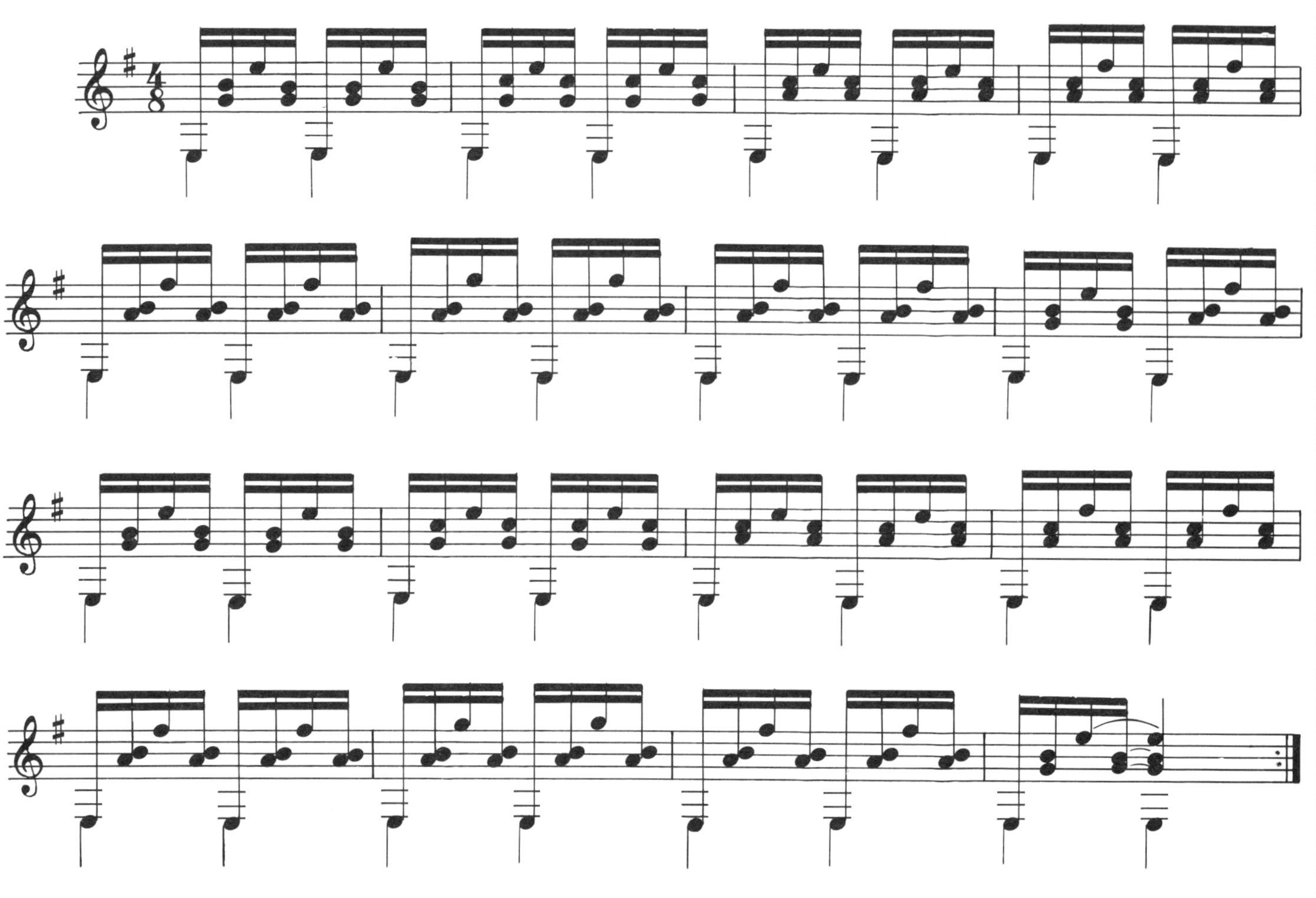

Now practice Exs. 40a and 40b in 3/8.

Thus, Ex. 40a becomes:

... and Ex. 40b becomes:

While Solo No. 18 provides further practice in right-hand finger alternation, it's also an etude for achieving further independence between 4 and 3. Previously, the reach of these two fingers has been limited to three strings. Solo No. 18 requires not only a reach across four strings, it also requires that you move 4 independently from 3. Thus, you're continuing to develop the coordination needed to minimize tension in your playing.

The up and down stemming of the half-note basses shouldn't confuse you. The two beams connecting the four upward stems indicate sixteenth values. Each measure should be counted as follows:

Solo No. 18

Cradle Song

S-H

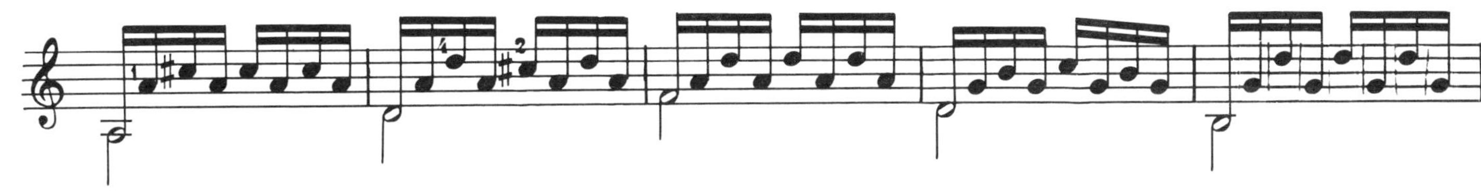

F (Fa) and G (So) on ⑥

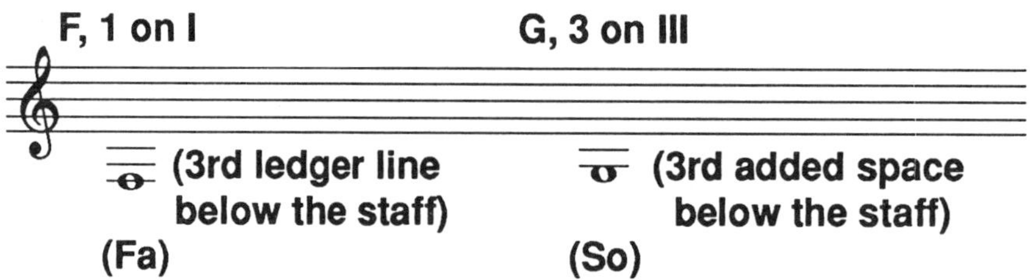

Ex. 41

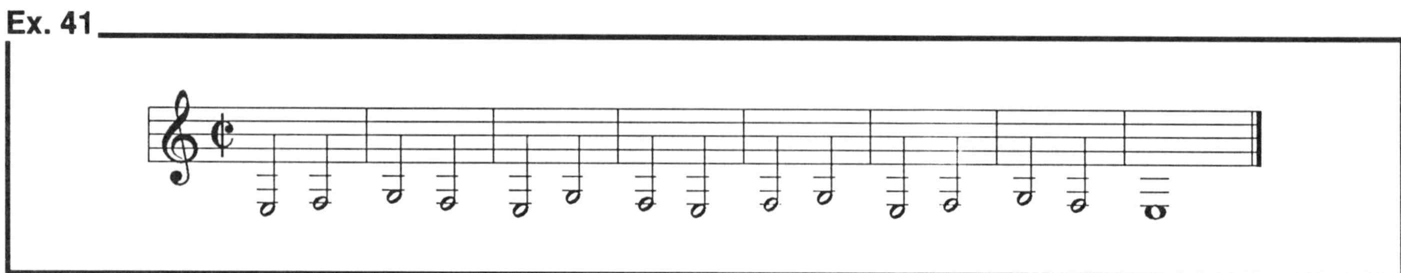

Calypso

Duet No. 24

S-H

Solos 19a, 19b, and 19c introduce p, i, a and its related figures (p, i, a, i and p, i, a, i, a, i). Before you begin, be sure you clearly understand the procedure for each of these figures, as described in *Part One,* p. 71. Carefully practice the figure found in each solo until you can execute it with reasonable fluency, then practice the solo.

Solo 19a

P, I, A Etude

A. S.

Solo No. 19b

P, I, A, I Etude

A. S.

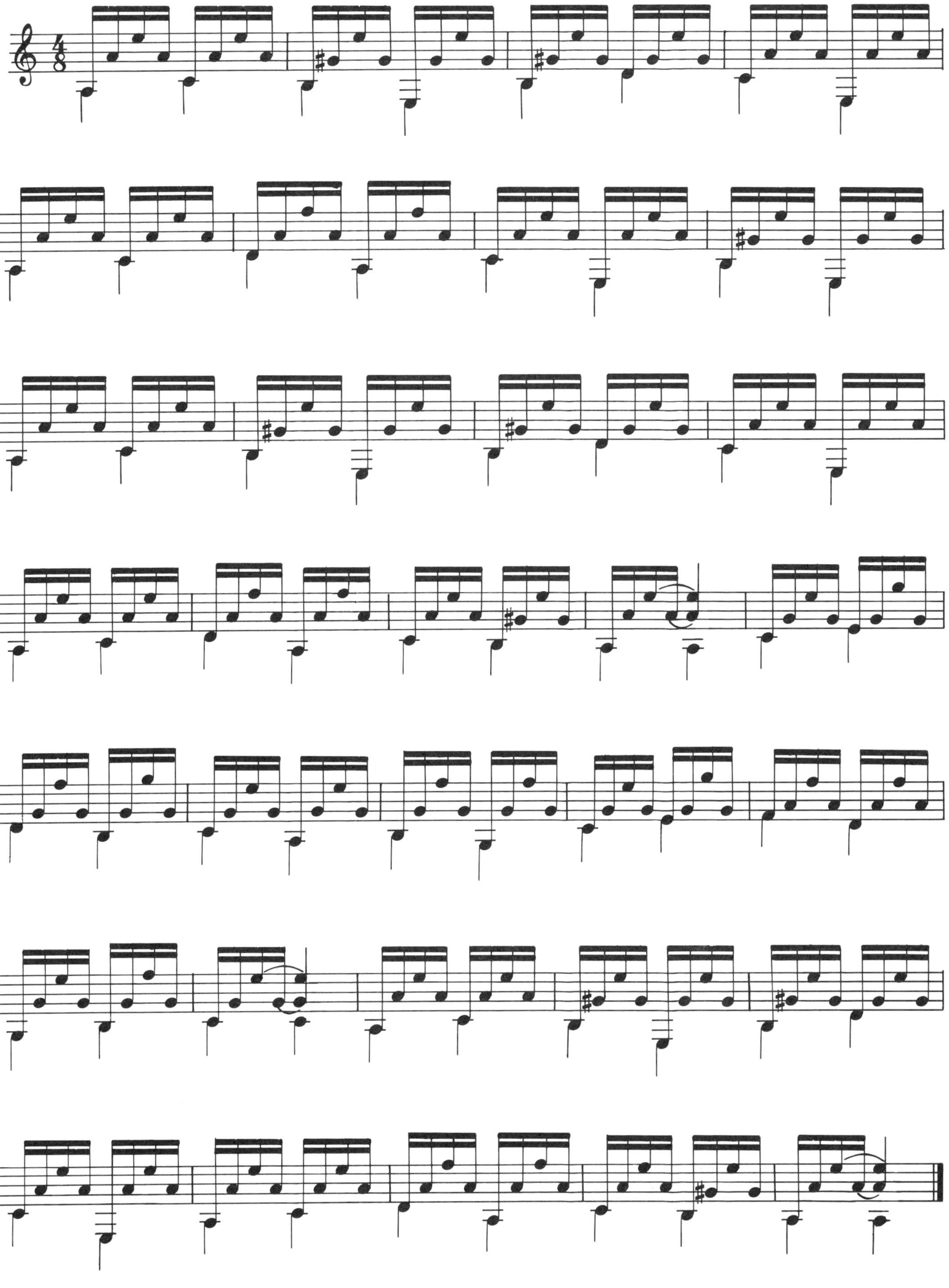

Solo No. 19c

P, I, A, I, A, I Etude

A. S.

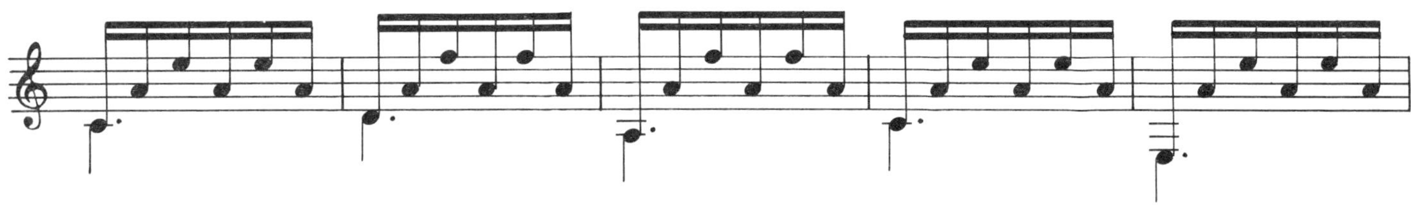

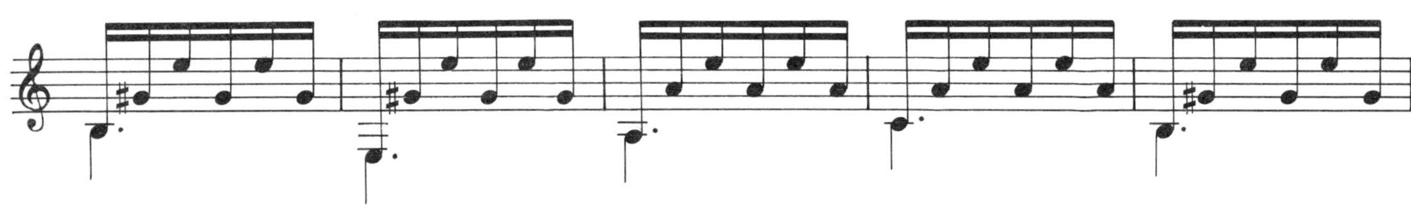

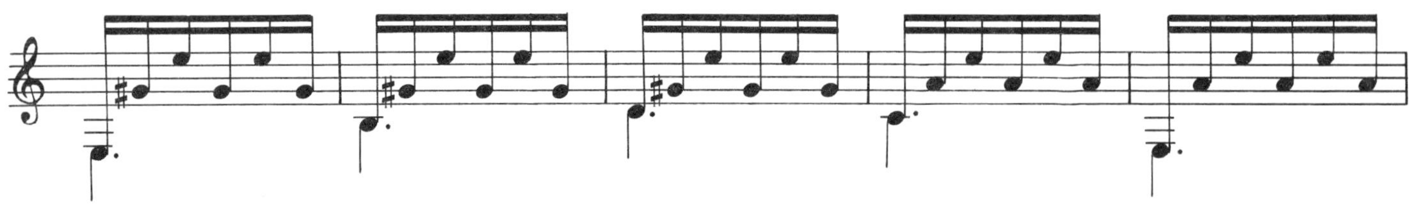

Besides giving you practice in reading lower notes, Solo No. 20 provides further training in alternation between p and i and between i and a.

Merry Dance

S-H

Solo No. 20

M.M. ♪= 104

Quintuple Meter

While not as common as duple, triple, or quadruple meter, quintuple meter is occasionally found in guitar music. It most frequently appears in contemporary music—usually as either 5/4 or 5/8 meter.

Solo No. 21 is your first encounter with quintuple meter. Before you begin to play, practice counting the following:

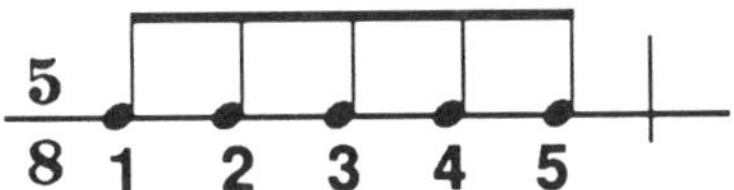

Carefully observe the A♭ (Le) on ③ at I, the D♯ (Ri) on ④ at I, and the F♯ (Fi) on ⑥ at II.

Theme and Variation

Solo No. 21

A. H.

M.M. ♪= 152

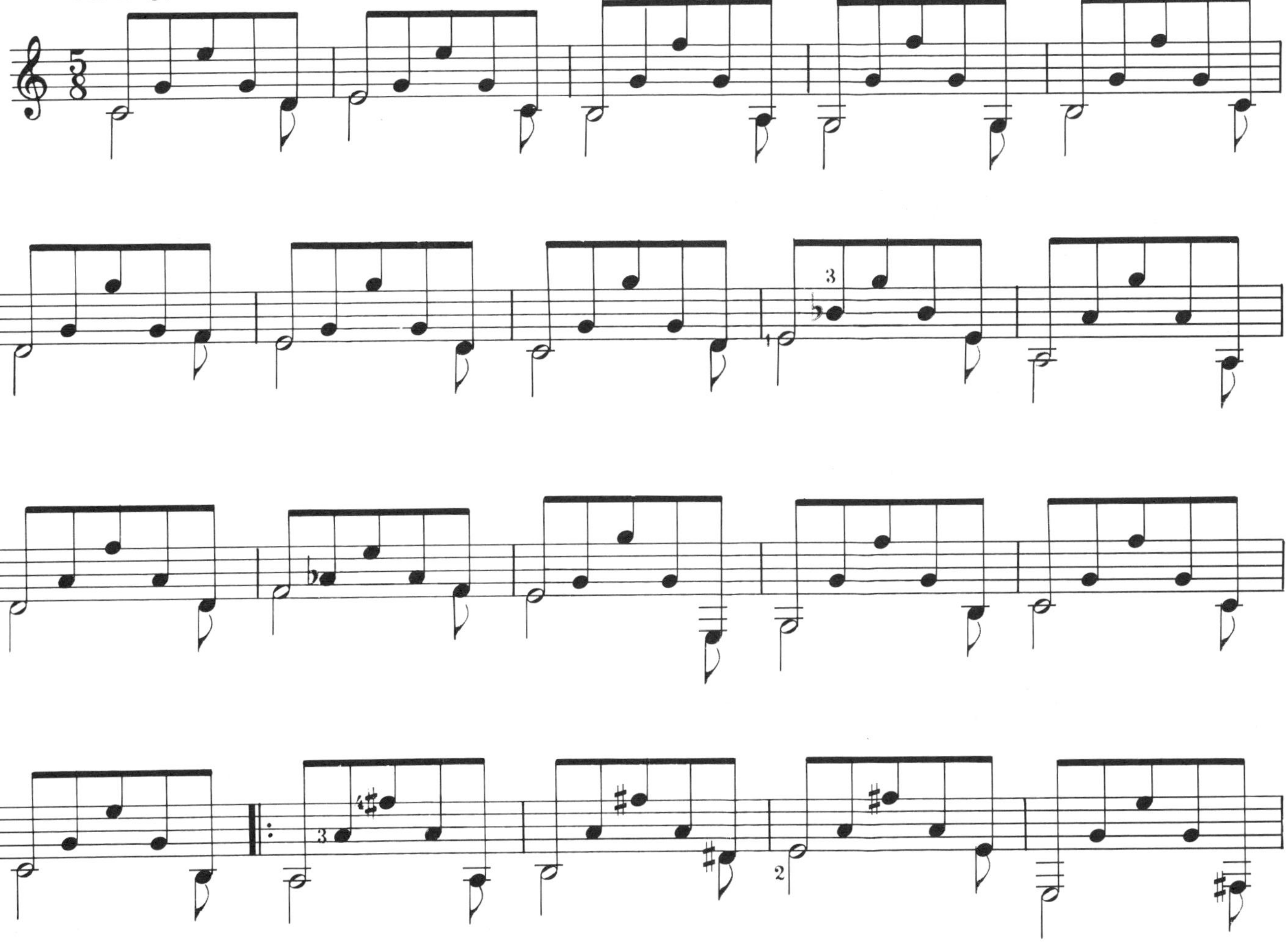

1.
2.
M.M. ♪= 126
p i m i a i

1.
2.
M.M. ♪= 126
p i m i a i

1.
2.

Alternation on a Single String

Solo No. 22 introduces alternation on a single string — a more challenging movement than alternation on adjacent strings. Be sure you understand the difference between the two movements before proceeding (see *Part One*, pp. 71 – 73). From the beginning of practice, aim to acquire habits of correct movement.

Notice the ***D.C. al Fine*** which occurs in the last measure of Solo No. 22. This is an abbreviation of "Da Capo al Fine" (Italian, pronounced "Dah **Kah**-poh al **Fee**-nay"), which means "from beginning to end." Thus, "D.C. al Fine" indicates that you go back to the beginning of the piece and play to the measure marked "Fine."

The *fermata* (Italian, "pause," pronounced "fair-**mah**-tah") is introduced in measures 16 and 32. A fermata, 𝄐 , over a note or rest means to hold that note or rest for longer than its written value. The duration of the fermata is left to the discretion of the performer. In Solo No. 22, however, it seems appropriate to increase the duration of the affected eighth notes to approximately twice their value. The only exception is when you reach the end of the piece at "Fine." Following a ritard begun in the next-to-the-last measure, you should allow the final note to sound for at least two added beats.

For now, use only i and m in Solo No. 22 — training m and a to sound a single string begins with Solo No. 24.

Single-String Alternation Etude I

A. H.

Solo No. 22

After practicing Solo No. 22 as written, add two more sixteenth notes to each measure and practice the piece as though it's written in 4/8 meter:

Solo No. 23 is another etude for developing alternation on a single string — now involving ① and ②. Carefully observe the A♯ (Li) on ⑤ (measure 18), formed with 1 at I.

Avoid confusion and error! Before you attempt to play the piece, carefully visualize and become familiar with all left-hand fingerings.

Single-String Alternation Etude II

S-H

Solo No. 23

As you did for Solo No. 22, practice Solo No. 23 in 4/8 meter, adding two sixteenth notes to each measure.

String Crossing

Solo No. 24 introduces string crossing — an extremely important facet of technique. String crossing involves shifting your right-hand position across adjacent strings. Your fluency as a guitarist depends on the accuracy and speed with which you can cross from one string to another (see *Part One*, pp. 74 – 76).

In each measure of Solo No. 24, you must shift your hand the distance of one string. After sounding ③ with i (the shorter finger) and ② with m, immediately shift your hand to place i in an optimum position for sounding ②. At the end of each measure, you must shift your hand back to its original position in preparation for beginning the next measure.

Before practicing Solo No. 24, visualize and become thoroughly familiar with all left-hand fingerings — this will allow you to give the fullest attention to crossing. (Note the key signature, which contains an F♯, and be sure to observe the E♭ (Me) on ④ at I.) It's also beneficial to carry out the string-crossing exercise explained in *Part One*, pp. 75 – 76, before playing this etude.

Solo No. 24

Crossing Etude I

S-H

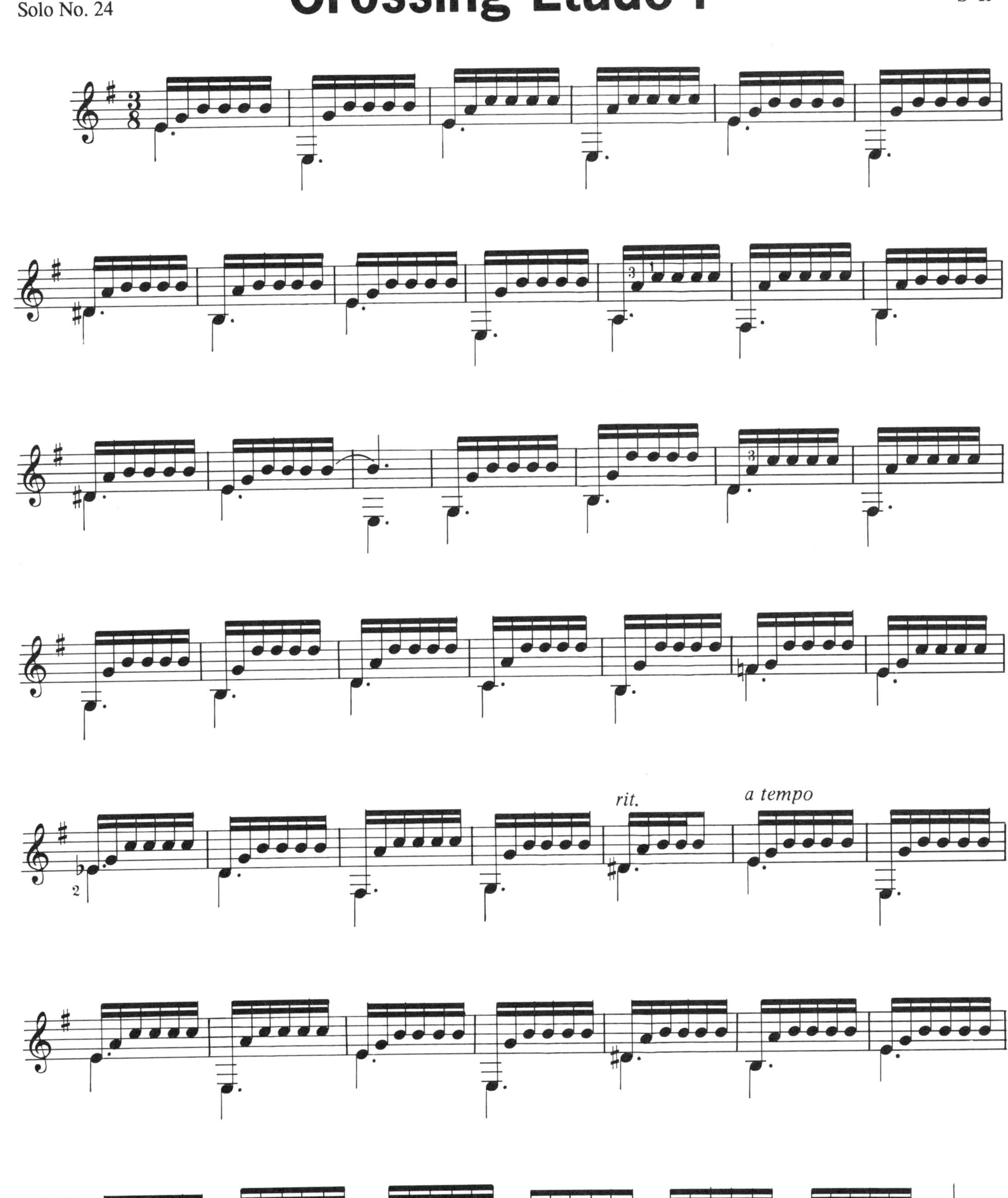

Now practice Solo No. 24 with m and a alternating on a single string. Since m and a have similar reaches, you don't need to shift your right hand when executing this figure with m and a (see *Part One*, p. 79). Although, during m and a alternation, Solo No. 24 doesn't involve string crossing, it's still a valuable exercise for training m and a.

As indicated in *Part One,* all exercises and pieces for i and m should eventually be practiced with m and a; m replaces i, and a replaces m.

Compound Meters

All the meters you've encountered so far are called simple meters. A ***simple meter*** is any meter in which the beat is represented either by one or more undotted values (2/4, 3/4, 4/4, 4/8), or no more than one dotted value (3/8).

Compound meter means that a dotted value (♩.) represents the beat, and that two or more of these values occur within each measure. Compound meters are classified according to the number of dotted values present in each measure.

Compound duple meter consists of two dotted values, which could be easily counted as shown:

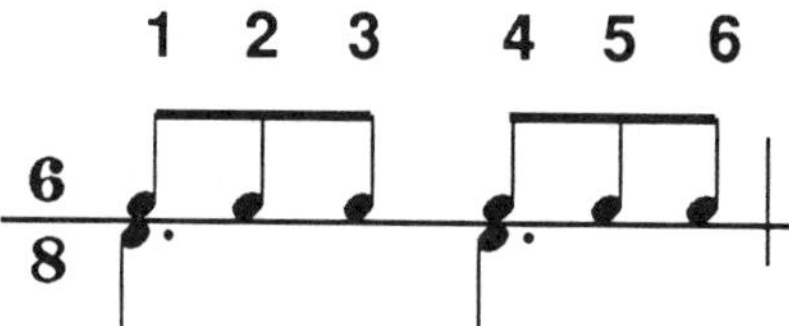

This manner of counting, however, doesn't express the number of pulses appearing in each measure. A more effective way of counting compound duple meter is to count the first two eighths of the pulse in the normal manner for counting eighths: "1, &." Then add "a" (pronounced "uh" as in "about") to account for the last eighth note of the pulse. Thus, you'll count 6/8 meter as follows:

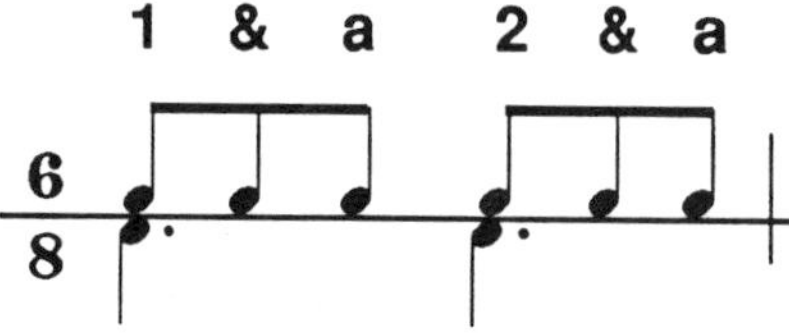

Compound triple meter consists of three dotted values:

Compound quadruple meter consists of four dotted values:

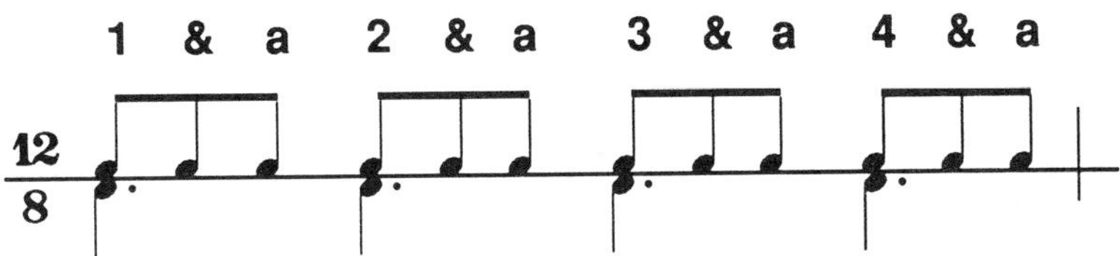

Directing groups of three at a slower tempo was explained on p. 71. At a more rapid tempo, the ↑ between "&" and "a" will naturally become less distinct. But this will cause no problem as long as your downbeat (↓) is clear.

The following example consists of the first two measures of Solo No. 24, now in 6/8 meter. As you practice this example, count aloud to establish groups of three. Then practice Solo No. 24 entirely in 6/8 meter. Continue counting aloud until you feel secure with compound duple meter.

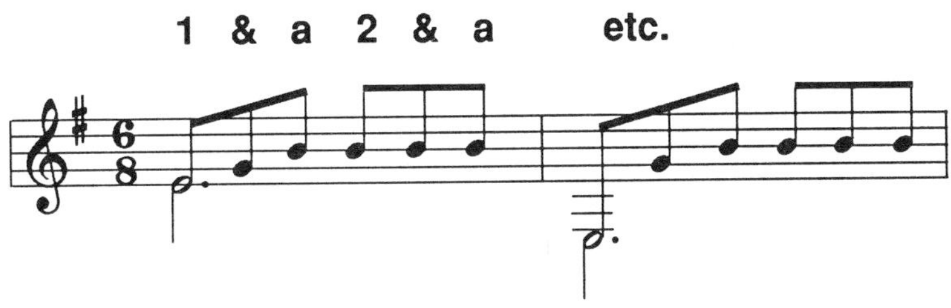

Playing consecutive groups of three notes with alternation may be confusing at first because you play the first note of each figure alternately with i, then m:

In the following example, the first measure of Solo No. 24 is rewritten in 9/8. Practice Solo No. 24 in 9/8 until fluent, carefully alternating i and m while counting aloud. This will help you maintain strict alternation in subsequent solos which contain consecutive groups of three notes played with the fingers.

Solo No. 25 is an etude for alternation on both single and adjacent strings. Once you've established the most advantageous joint positions for m and i alternation in sounding ③, maintain these joint positions as you shift to ②. *Don't reach for* ② *with i!* Rather, you should shift your forearm from the elbow the instant before i sounds ②.

Solo No. 25

Crossing Etude II

S - H

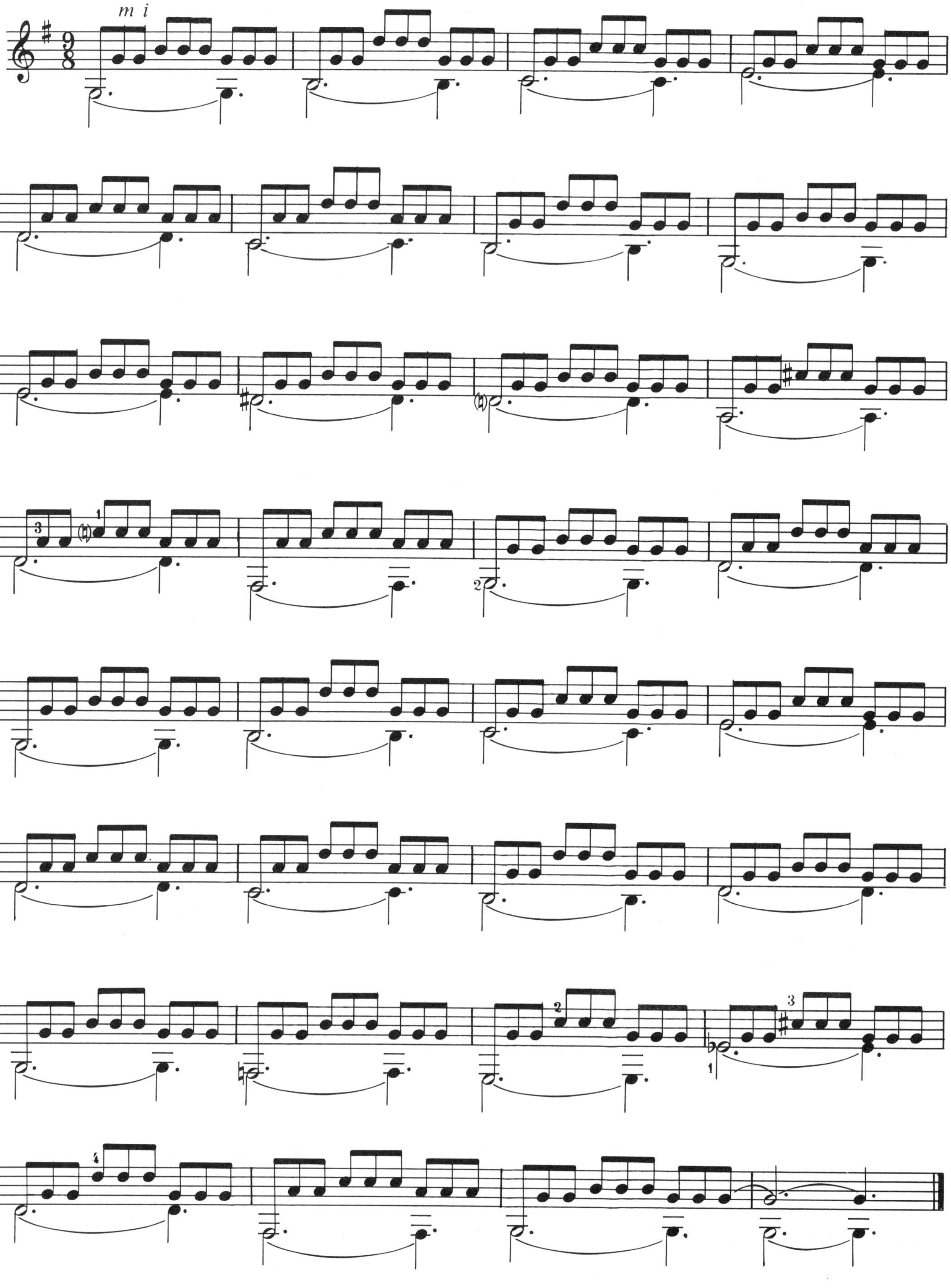

Solo No. 26 requires three successive shifts to higher strings followed by three shifts back to the starting position.

Solo No. 26

Crossing Etude III

A. S.

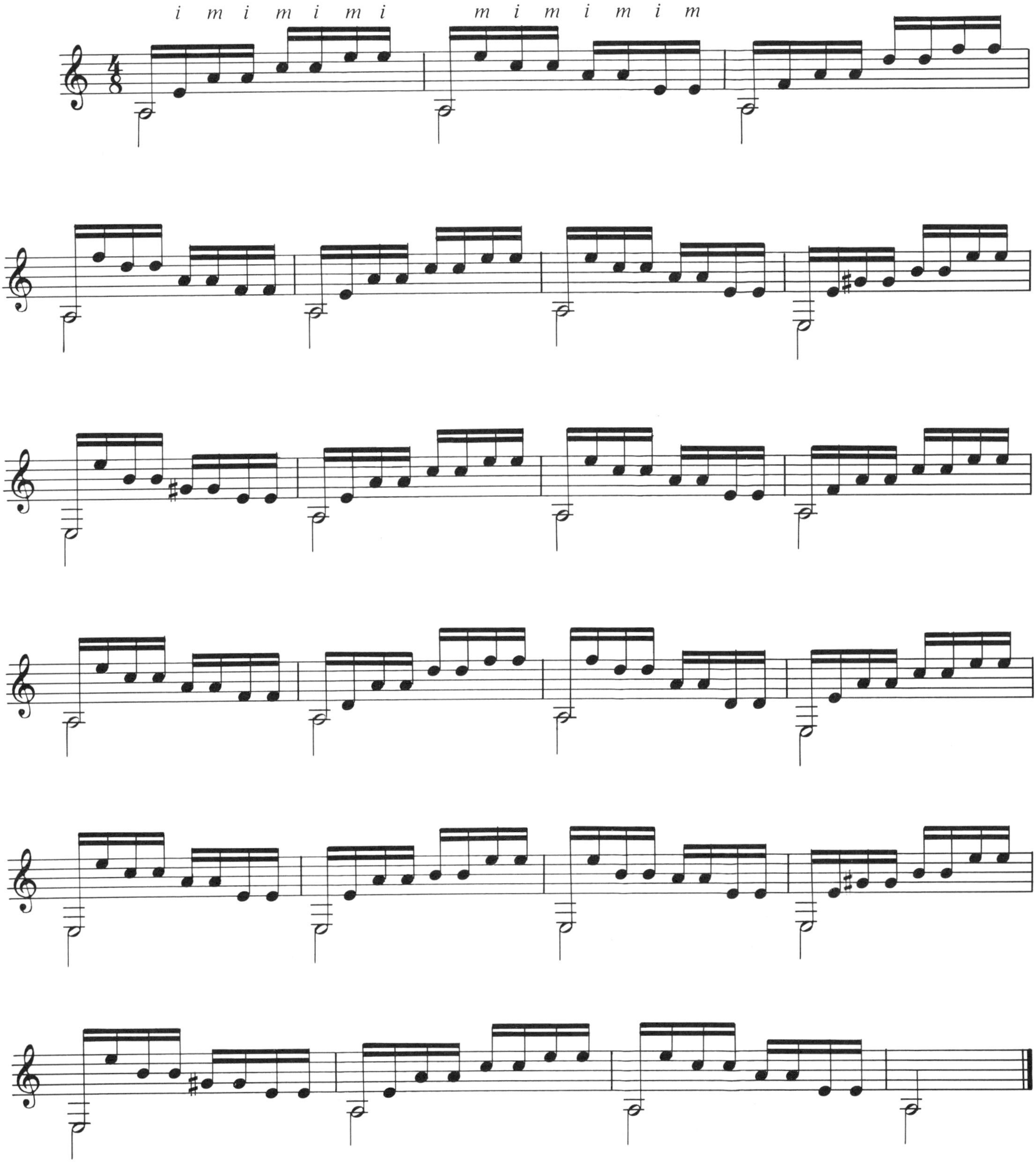

i m i m i m i m i m i m i m

Perhaps you've noticed that, in all the previous string crossing etudes, m has led in crossing to the higher string, and i has led in crossing to the lower string. Because of the differing reaches of i and m, this procedure feels more secure in beginning string crossing. But, in playing scales and other passages involving strict alternation and string crossing, it's not always practical to lead to the higher string with m and to the lower string with i. Thus, you also need to practice string crossing with the order of leading reversed, so that i leads to the higher string and m leads to the lower string. Solo No. 27 provides you with an opportunity to practice this important facet of right-hand training.

Solo No. 27

Crossing Etude IV

S - H

Once you've practiced single shifts with i leading to the higher string and m to the lower string, you should then practice three shifts in each direction, using the same order of leading in string crossing. Solo No. 28 is an altered version of Solo No. 26. Cultivate smooth and precise shifts as you practice.

Solo No. 28

Crossing Etude V

A. S.

Playing Scales

Scale passages pose a special problem in string crossing. The notes of major scales across the fingerboard occur three notes per string on five of the strings and two notes on the remaining string. Alternating two fingers to sound three notes per string requires that you shift to each adjacent string with a different finger. Thus, you need to practice this procedure on open strings, carefully watching your hand and maintaining a consistently firm stroke in sounding each string:

Ex. 42

Since you're familiar with all the natural notes in the open position, you'll begin with the ***Complete Open-Position C-Major Scale Form.***† This succession of notes consists of a complete one-octave C-major scale, plus four notes above to G (So) on ① at III and five notes below to E (Mi) on the open sixth string. To focus more fully on training your right hand, you should memorize the complete open-position C-major scale form before playing it on the guitar.

Proceed as follows with Ex. 43:

- ❑ **Set aside the guitar. Beginning with the lowest C (Do on ⑤), read and say the solfege syllable and finger number for each successive note of Ex. 43 in the following manner: Do-3, Re-0 ("oh" for open), Mi-2, Fa-3, So-0, La-2, etc. Maintain a steady rhythm, and clearly visualize each finger and each open string as though you're actually playing the notes.**

- ❑ **When you can do this easily, carry out the procedure from memory until you can maintain a flowing pace without hesitations. Then take the guitar and prepare to play.**

- ❑ **Close your eyes and carefully play the scale, using free-stroke alternation. Continue to solfege each note. Also, clearly visualize and feel the placement of each left-hand finger. Begin slowly at first. When you can play the scale securely, accelerate the tempo until you can play at about M.M. ♩ = 80 without hesitation.**

†***Open position*** indicates that open strings are used and that the left hand is in position for the first finger to play the 1st fret.

- ❑ **When your left hand feels secure, practice the scale form while watching your right hand. Establish a feeling of precise alternation and string crossing. *Emphasize accurate rhythms and evenness of volume between tones.***

Ex. 43

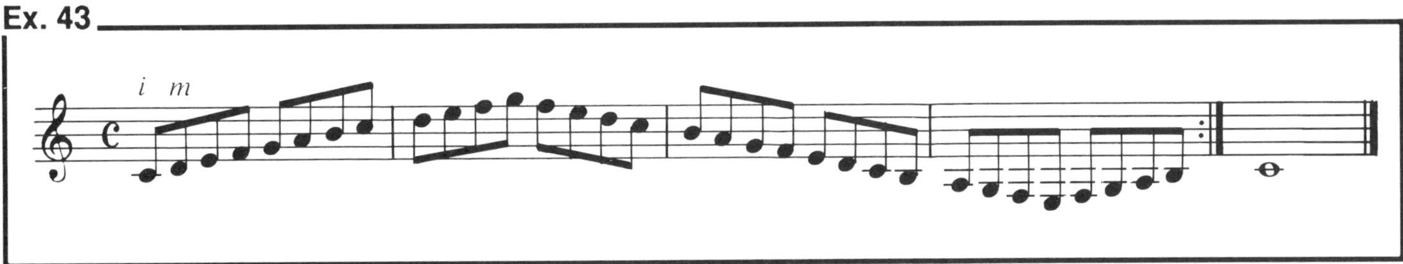

Ex. 44 is a reading exercise. First scan the exercise to determine its general shape and design. Solfege and visualize before playing. Then practice slowly and accurately. ***Avoid confusion and error!*** Use the metronome, and gradually increase the tempo as you become secure with alternation, string crossing, and tone production.

Ex. 44

Rest-Stroke Alternation

Before proceeding, see *Part One,* "Comparing Rest-Stroke and Free-Stroke," p. 86, and "Rest-Stroke Finger Alternation," pp. 87 – 88. All considerations regarding string crossing when playing free-stroke also apply in rest-stroke.

Ex. 45

Now reverse the order of fingering in Ex. 45 to begin with m. This changes the finger you'll use at the points of string crossing.

When you can play Ex. 45 with a satisfactory tone while maintaining secure string crossing, practice Exs. 42 and 43 with rest-stroke. Then practice Ex. 44 with rest-stroke. Again, practicing familiar exercises allows you to give more attention to tone production, string crossing, and evenness of rhythm and volume.

Solo No. 29

Danza in C

S-H

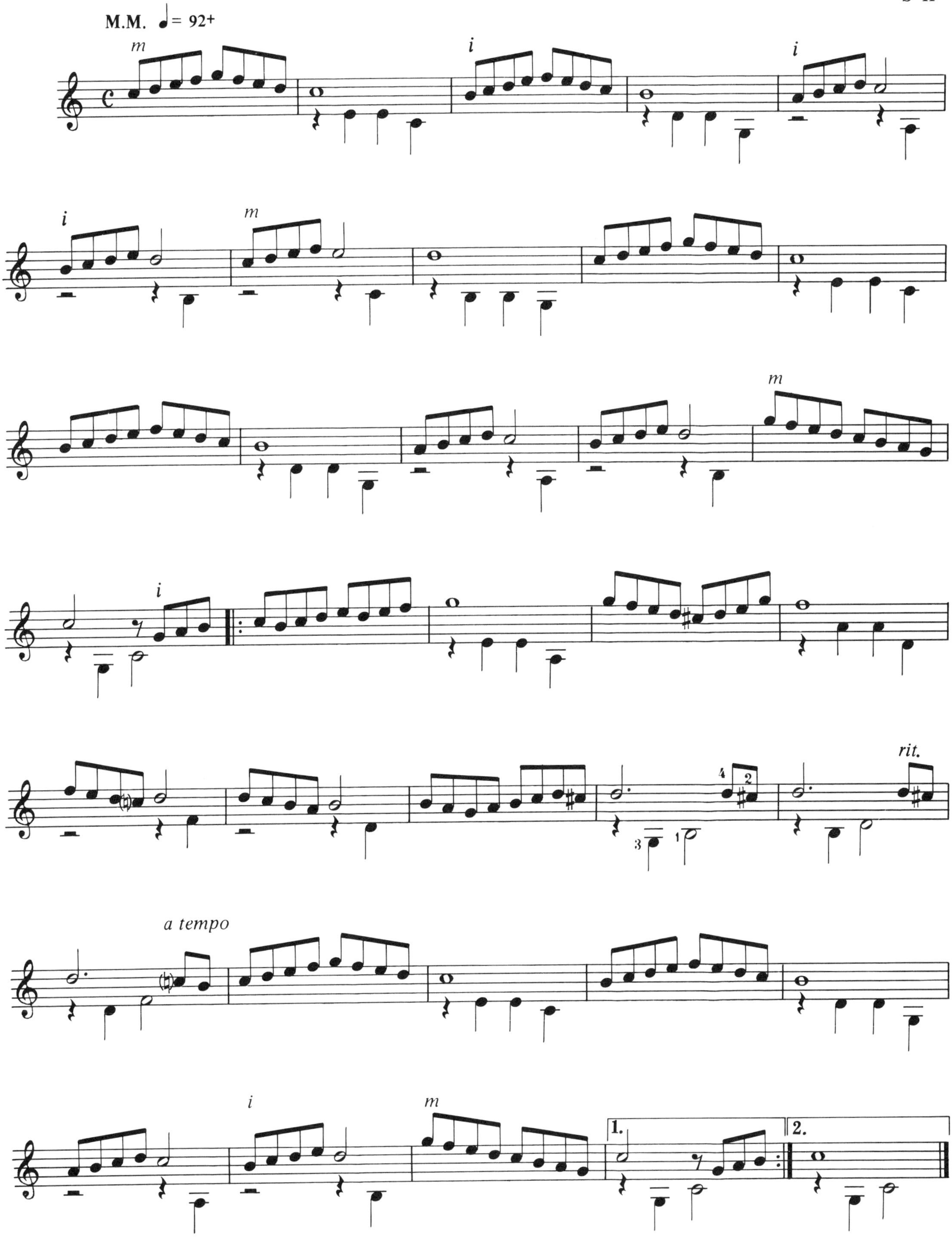

M.M. ♩ = 92+

m *i* *i*

i *m*

m

i

rit.

a tempo

i *m* 1. 2.

Notice the term *poco* (Italian, meaning "little") in measure 8 of Duet 25. "Poco rit." means that you should only slightly ritard the tempo.

Sonatina in C

Duet No. 25

A. H.

rit.
a tempo
1.
2.
BII ④

Duet No. 26

Arietta

A. H.

M.M. ♩= 80

(This page is left blank to avoid a page turn in the following piece.)

Duet No. 27

Baroque Reflections

A. H.

M.M. ♩. = 66+

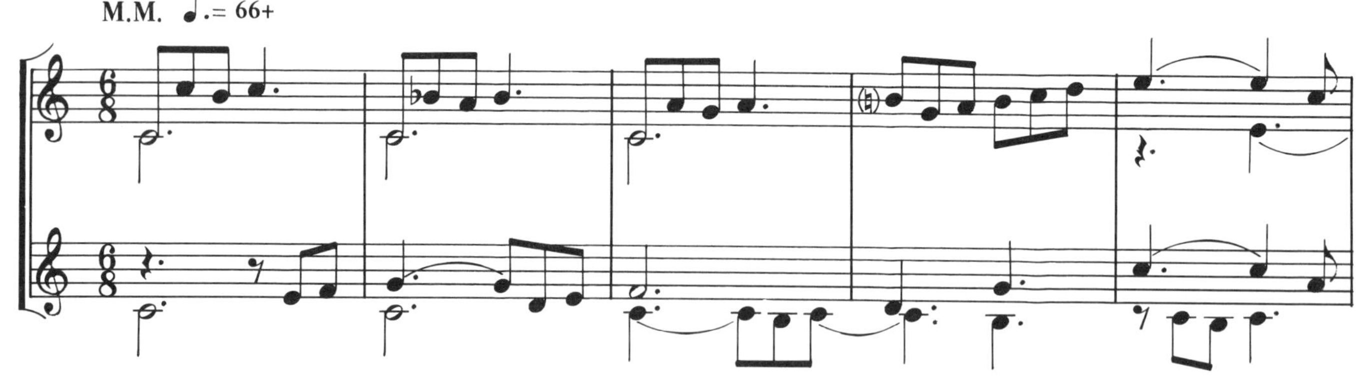

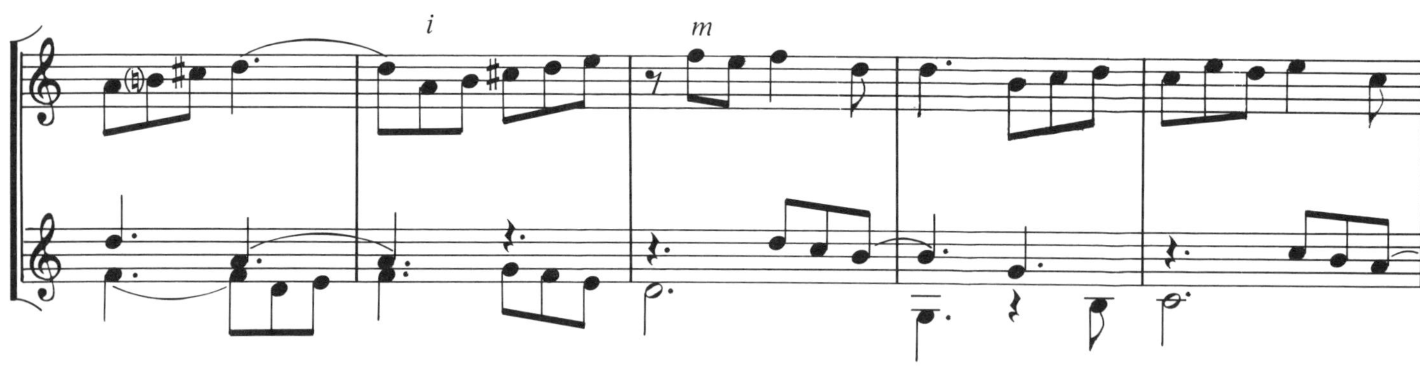

m i
2
2

Playing Chords with P and the Fingers

Sounding strings simultaneously with p and the fingers poses special problems of muscular coordination. See *Part One*, pp. 88 – 89, for an explanation of this important facet of technical development.

Avoid confusion and error! Before playing, acquire habits of accuracy by clearly visualizing each left-hand finger formation at a slow and even tempo.

Ex. 46

Solo No. 30

Chanson

A. H.

Notice that Solo No. 31 begins with the third beat preceding the first bar line. This is commonly called an ***upbeat.*** You should begin Solo No. 31 by counting a complete measure of three beats and begin to play on the count of "3." Notice also that this extra beat is accounted for in the final measure, which contains only two beats.

Solo No. 31

Pavane

A. H.

Sounding Two Notes Together with P and One Finger Free-Stroke

From the standpoint of tone production, many students find this technique more challenging than moving p–i–m together. Before proceeding, review *Part One*, p. 89.

First, practice Ex. 47 with p–i until you're reasonably secure. Then practice with p–m, and then with p–a.

Ex. 47

Ex. 48 is a variation of Ex. 47 and involves alternation in playing repeated eighth notes. First practice p–i together on the beat alternating with m off the beat. Then practice p–m alternating with i. Then carry out the same procedure with p–m alternating with a, and finally p–a alternating with m.

Ex. 48

In Solo No. 32, the quarter rest between the upper and lower voices (as in the first measure) indicates the presence of a middle voice — the half note which follows completes the metric value of that voice for the measure.

Rustic Idyl

Solo No. 32

S - H

Solo No. 33 continues your right-hand alternation training. It's also a piece for developing further independence and coordination between the third and fourth fingers of your left hand. You've already practiced reaching across four strings with these two fingers (Solo No. 18) — now you'll practice reaching across five strings.

Be sure to observe the B♭ (Te) on ⑤ at I.

Solo No. 33

Minuet

S-H

Solo No. 34

Catalonian Folk Song†

A. H.

†This piece is based on a folk tune from Felipe Pedrell's *Cancionero Musical Popular Español*, 2nd ed. (1918; rpt. Barcelona: Boileau, 1958).

The Complete Open-Position G-Major Scale Form

The *Complete Open-Position G-Major Scale Form* spans two octaves, plus an extension of two lower notes on the sixth string. The F♯ in the key signature presents you with one new note on the fingerboard: F♯ (Fi) on ④ at IV, played with the fourth finger. Thus, you'll begin training 4 for playing notes on the 4th fret.

Using rest-stroke, practice each figure in Ex. 49 until you can place 4 close to the 4th fret with accuracy and security. Keep the joints of 4 (particularly the middle joint) sufficiently flexed within their midranges — don't allow the joints to collapse as you press the string against the fret.

Ex. 49

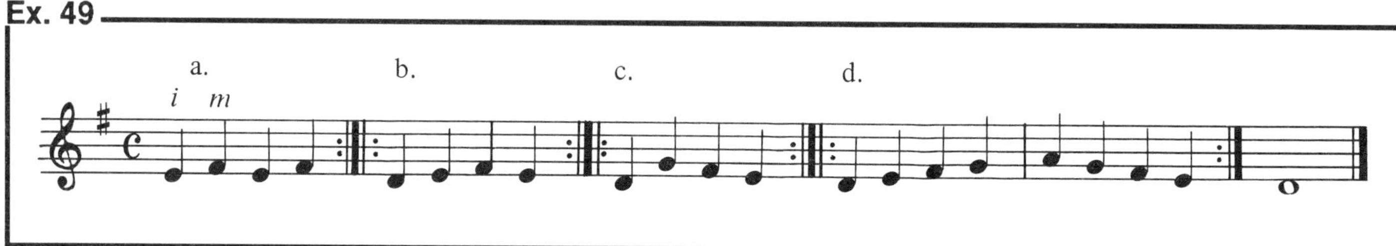

Using the visualization procedure, memorize and play the following complete open-position G-major scale form. Again, use rest-stroke.†

Ex. 50

†To achieve a desirable balance of development between rest-stroke and free-stroke, begin emphasizing rest-stroke when practicing scale exercises.

Ex. 51 — A Reading Exercise

Ex. 52 — A Reading Exercise

Duet No. 28

Sonatina in G

A. H.

i
m
3
3

Ballade

Solo No. 35

A. H.

1
2

Papillon

Duet No. 29

A. H.

(This page is left blank to avoid a page turn in the following piece.)

Further Development of Chords and Arpeggios

Solo No. 36a contains the p, i, m, a arpeggio. Prepare i–m–a as p flexes; m moves sympathetically with i, and a moves sympathetically with m; prepare p as a flexes.

Etude in E Minor

Solo No. 36a

S-H

After practicing Solo No. 36a, add one descending note to each arpeggio:

Solo No. 36b

This requires you to execute one opposed and one sympathetic movement with m.

Now practice this etude using the p, i, m, a, m, i figure (see *Part One,* p. 90). Carefully execute the opposed and sympathetic movements. In the descending part of the arpeggio, prepare m–i as a flexes.

Solo No. 36c

(This page is left blank to avoid an awkward page turn in the following piece.)

Berceuse

Duet No. 30

A. H.

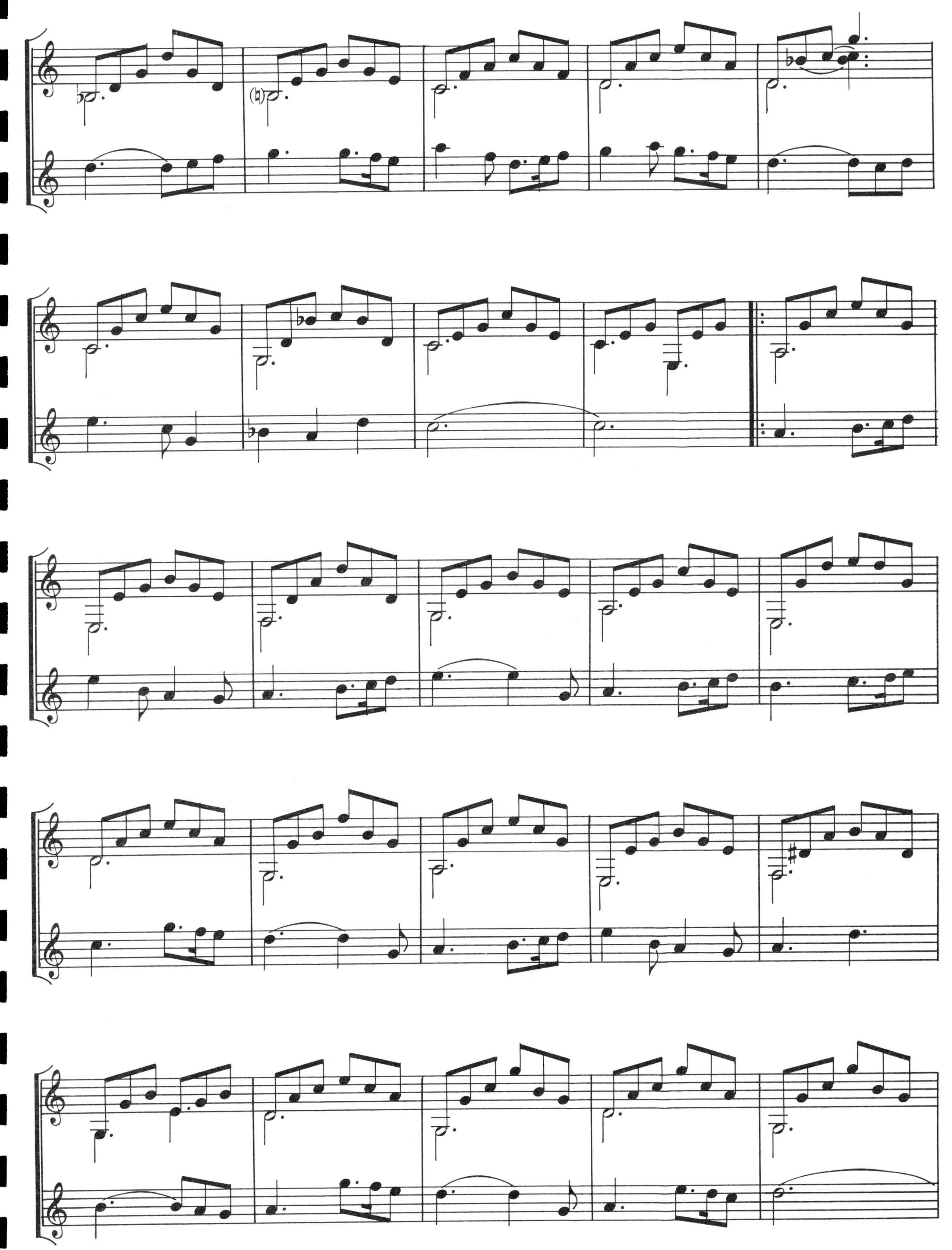

1.
2.
rit.

Hemiola

Hemiola (pronounced "hee-mee-**oh**-la") refers to the appearance of two pulses of equal duration within a measure of triple meter:

... or three pulses of equal duration within a measure of compound duple meter:†

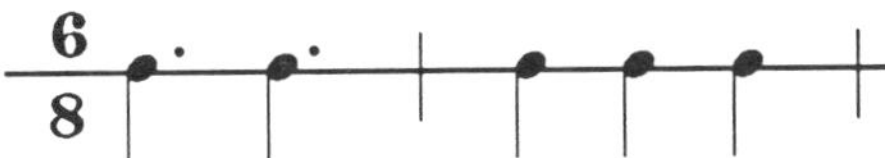

To accurately count a hemiola rhythm, determine the largest common value into which both the beat and the pulse forming the hemiola can be subdivided. For example, in the following measures:

...the largest common subdivision is the sixteenth. You can maintain the feeling of counting in sixteenths during the hemiola by simply adding "a" (pronounced "uh") to the normal count:

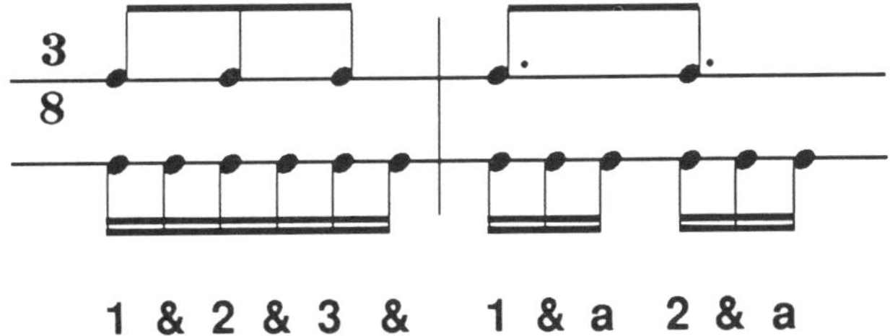

†For an explanation of compound duple meter, see p. 104.

Solo No. 37 is your introduction to hemiola. For example, observe measures 6 – 8:

Notice that measure 7 contains a hemiola rhythm — the two dotted eighth bass notes indicate that there are two pulses within this measure. Thus, you should count measures 6 – 8 as follows:

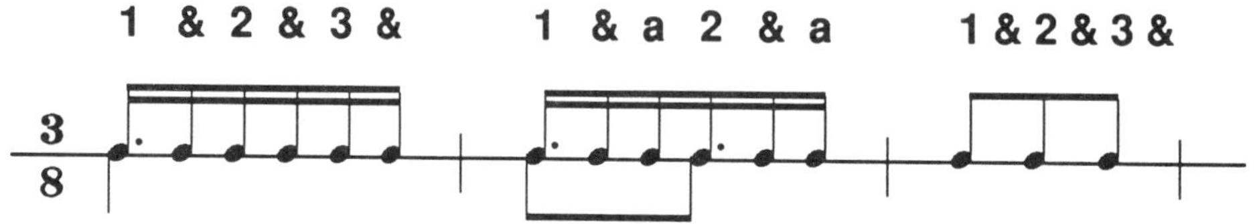

Be sure to observe the A♯ (Li) on ③ at III in measure 34.

NOTE: Although a metronome setting is provided for Solo No. 37, you shouldn't use the metronome as you practice this piece. Setting the metronome to click three beats per measure would be confusing during the hemiola measures. Thus, the metronome setting is intended only to provide you with a tempo.

Solo No. 37

Arabesque

A. H.

Mixed Meter

Mixed meter refers to music in which more or less frequent changes of time signature occur — most often this occurs in contemporary music. The main challenge in playing a mixed-meter piece is to be alert to the meter changes. Counting mixed meter, however, presents no special problems — you should count each meter in the normal manner.

Solo No. 38

Farewell

A.H.

rit.
a tempo
poco rit.
a tempo
rit.

Musette

Duet No. 31

A. H.

BII
i m a
1.
2.

Duet No. 32

Traveler's Song

A. H.

m
m
m
i
rit.

Chords of Four Notes

In sounding chords of four notes (p–i–m–a), you should concentrate on the firm placement and flexion of a. Give special attention to bringing out the highest note of each chord, which in Solo No. 39 is also the melody.

You should separately practice measure 8, which introduces a new challenge of independence between the third and fourth fingers. If any other left-hand fingering presents a challenge, isolate and practice that fingering until you can execute it easily. Aim for an even execution and a feeling of security as you change from one chord to the next.

Solo No. 39

Alla Marcia

A. S.

M.M. ♩= 72

(This page is left blank to avoid a page turn in the following piece.)

Duet No. 33

Bagatelle

A. H.

M.M. ♩= 80

1.
2.

Entrada

Solo No. 40

A. H.

(This page is left blank to avoid a page turn in the following piece.)

Duet No. 34

Elegy

A. H.

M.M. ♩ = 80

BII
BII

Solos No. 41 and No. 42 are based on the a, m, i arpeggio. They begin your introduction to the five arpeggios without p — an extremely important facet of your right-hand development. *Before you proceed, be sure you clearly understand the finger movements involved in the a, m, i arpeggio.* Carefully review the explanation in *Part One*, p. 100.

In Solo No. 41, you should stabilize your right hand by resting p on ⑤. Be sure to observe the D♭ (Ra) on ② at II, found in measure 30.

Solo No. 41

A, M, I Etude I

A. H.

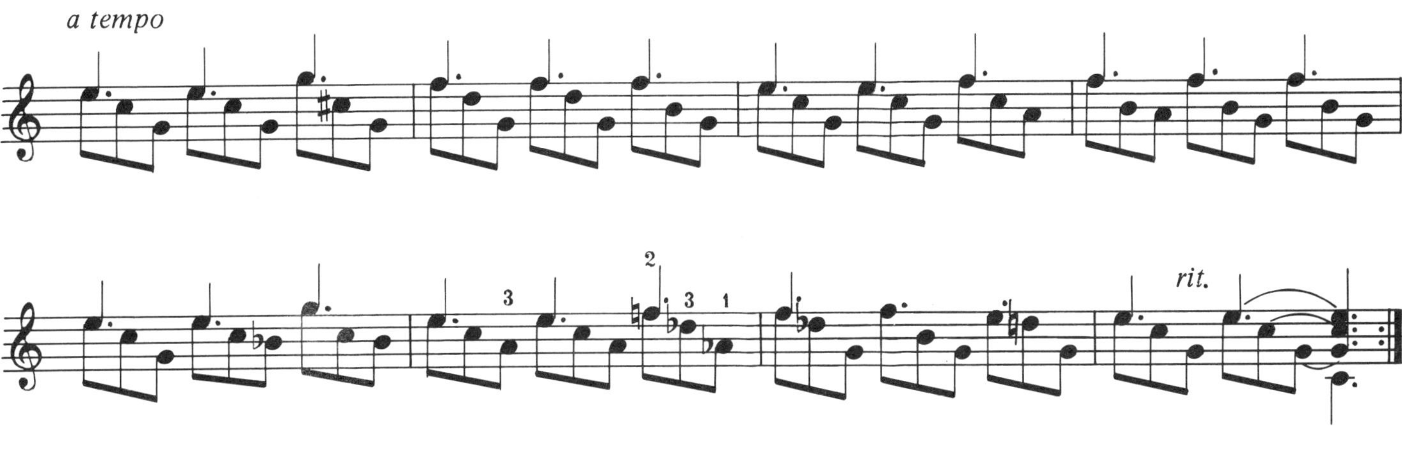

Triplets

In Solo 42, you'll encounter notes written as follows: . Notes written in this manner are called eighth-note triplets. A ***triplet*** indicates that three notes are played in the time normally occupied by one note of the next highest value. Thus, indicates that three eighth notes are played in the time normally occupied by one quarter value.

Composers generally use triplets to simplify the notation. For example, although measures 7 and 8 of Solo 42 could be written in 9/8:

... the long notes are easier to write in 3/4, using triplets to notate the arpeggios:

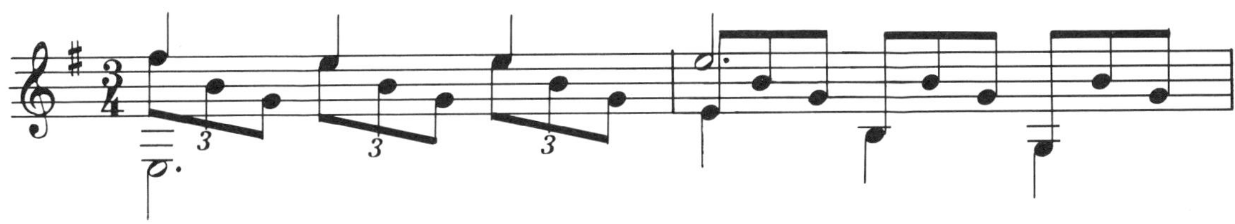

Eighth-note triplets are counted in the following manner:

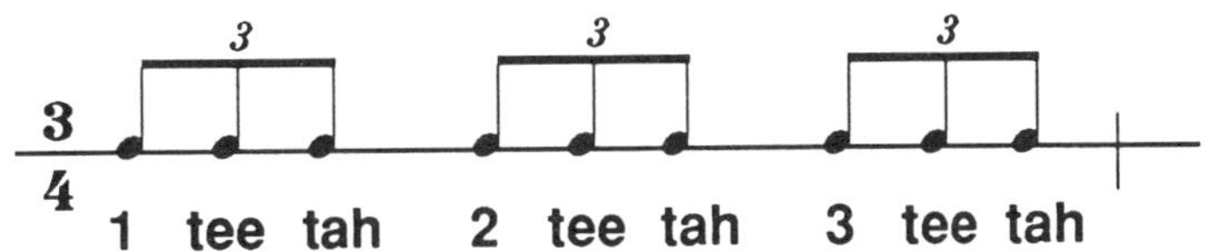

In Solo No. 42, you must now sound bass notes with p. Thus, you can no longer stabilize your hand by resting p on a string.

Solo No. 42

A, M, I Etude II

A. S.

Technical Slurs

Ex. 53 introduces the technical slur. You'll find information concerning this aspect of left-hand training in *Part One*, pp. 97 – 99. Practice each measure separately, then practice them in succession.

Ex. 53

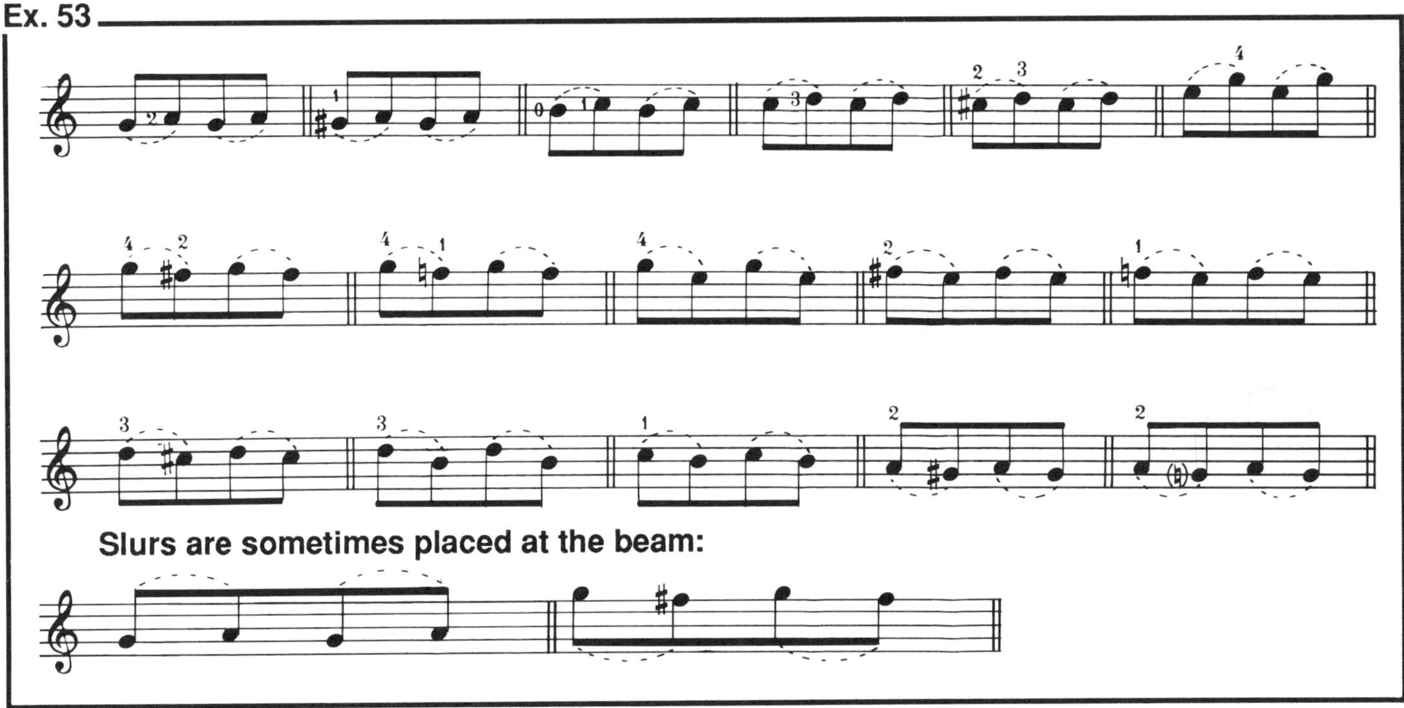

Duet No. 35

Gently Flowing

S. H.

M.M. ♩= 126

2
2

Solo No. 43

English Dance

A. H.

M.M. ♩ = 176+

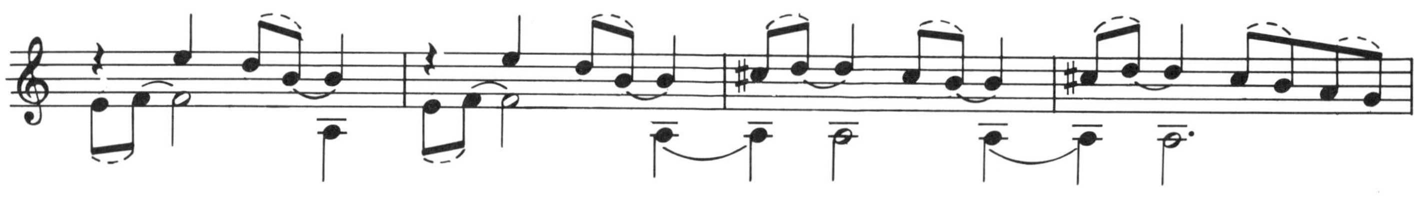

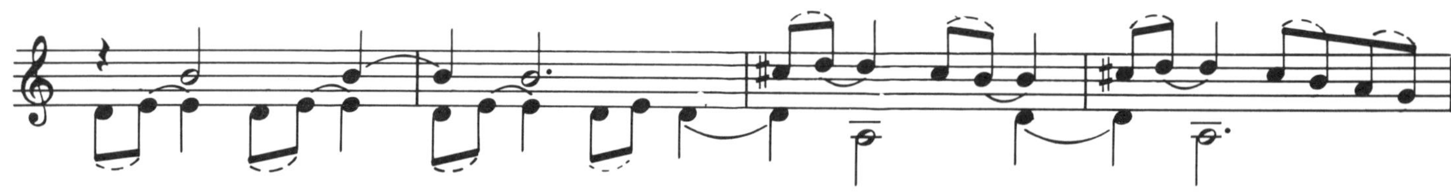

Solo No. 44 continues your progressive development of independence between the third and fourth fingers. While holding 1, 2, and 3 firmly on their respective strings, you must repeatedly reach with 4 to an adjacent fret and also the next lower string from the one held down by 3.

Solo No. 44

Serenata

S-H

M.M. ♩ = 88

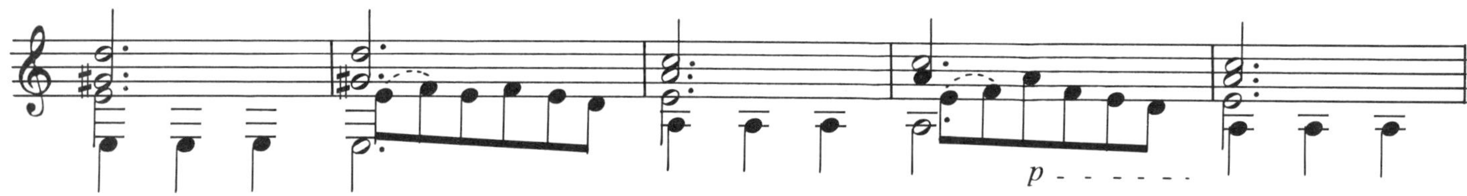

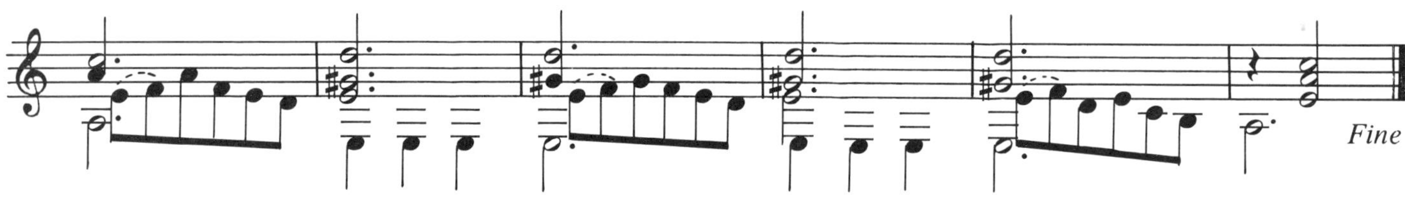

Solos No. 45 and No. 46 introduce a, i, m — the second of the five arpeggios without p. Again, before you begin to play, be sure you clearly understand the finger movements involved in this arpeggio. You'll find an explanation of a, i, m in *Part One*, pp. 102 – 103.

Solo No. 45

A, I, M Etude I

A. H.

Solo No. 46

A, I, M Etude II

A. S.

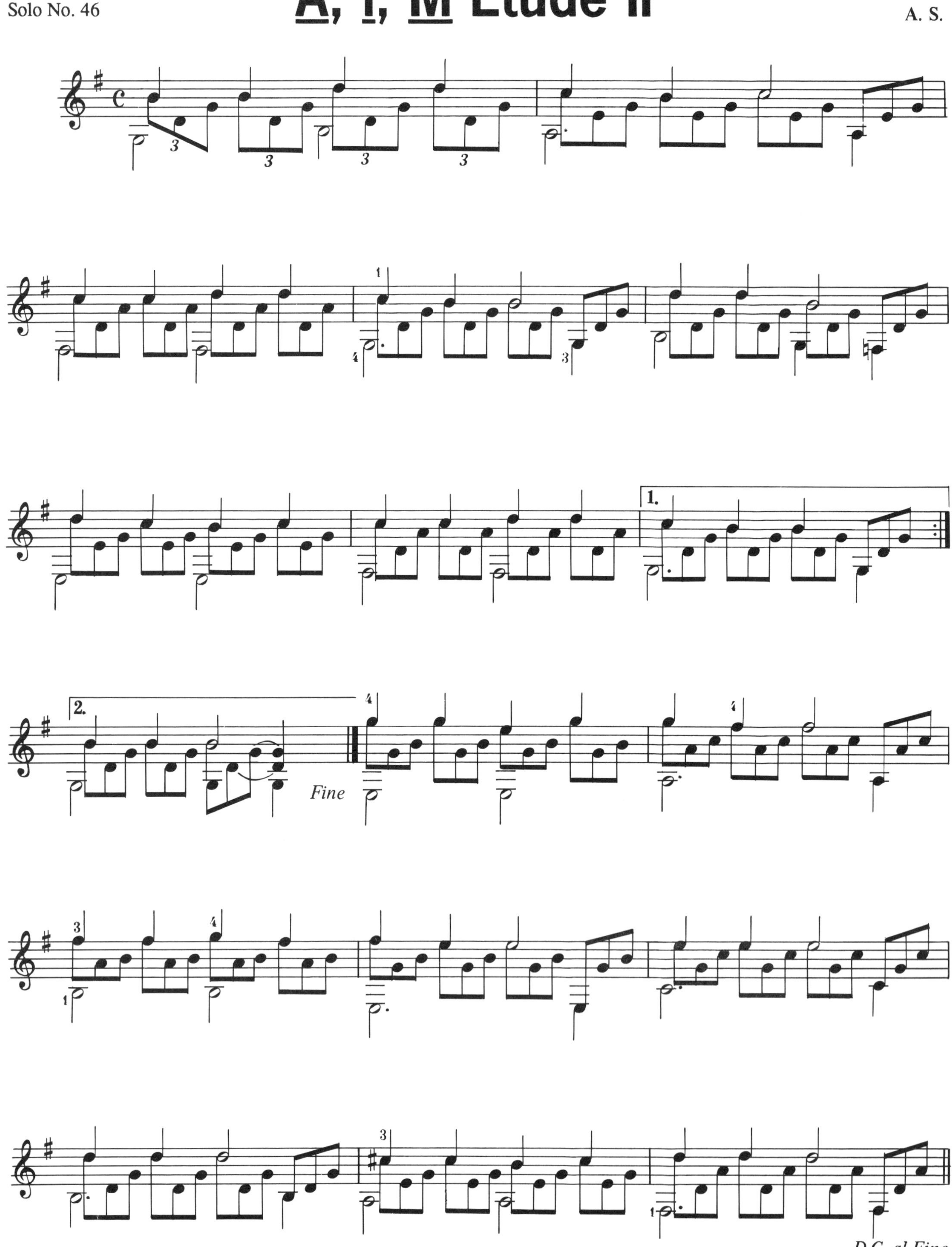

The Complete Open-Position D-Major Scale Form

The *Complete Open-Position D-Major Scale Form* contains a one-octave major scale and extensions of three notes above and six notes below. The C♯ found in the key signature (along with F♯) introduces a new note on the fifth string: C♯ (Di) formed at IV with the fourth finger. Having already used the fourth finger at IV on the fourth string, you should be able to form C♯ on the fifth string with relative ease. Avoid the tendency of the middle joint to collapse — keep both the middle and tip joints flexed in their midrange positions.

Carefully practice each figure in Ex. 54 until you can securely place 4 precisely on the string and close to the fret.

Ex. 54

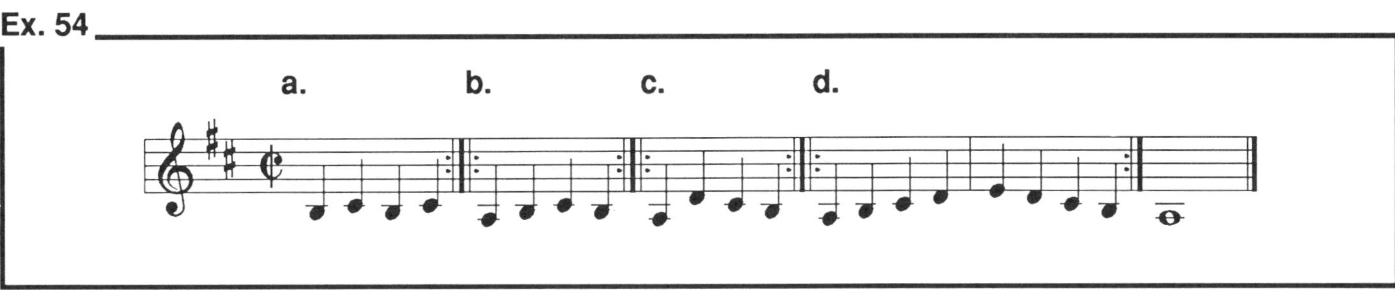

Through visualization, memorize and play the following complete open-position D-major scale form.

Ex. 55

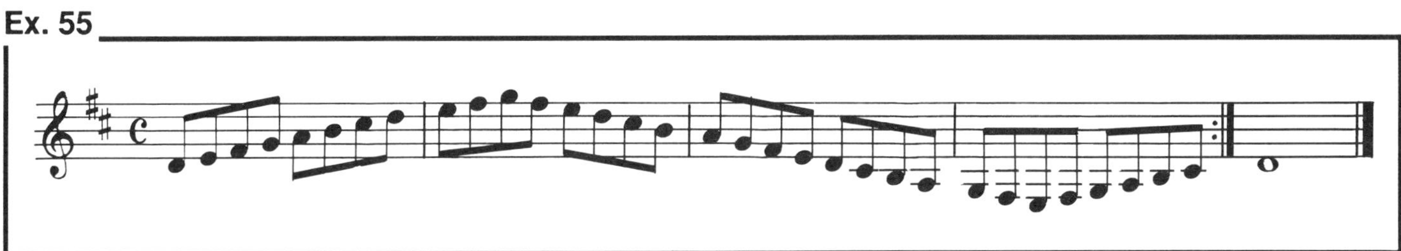

Ex. 56

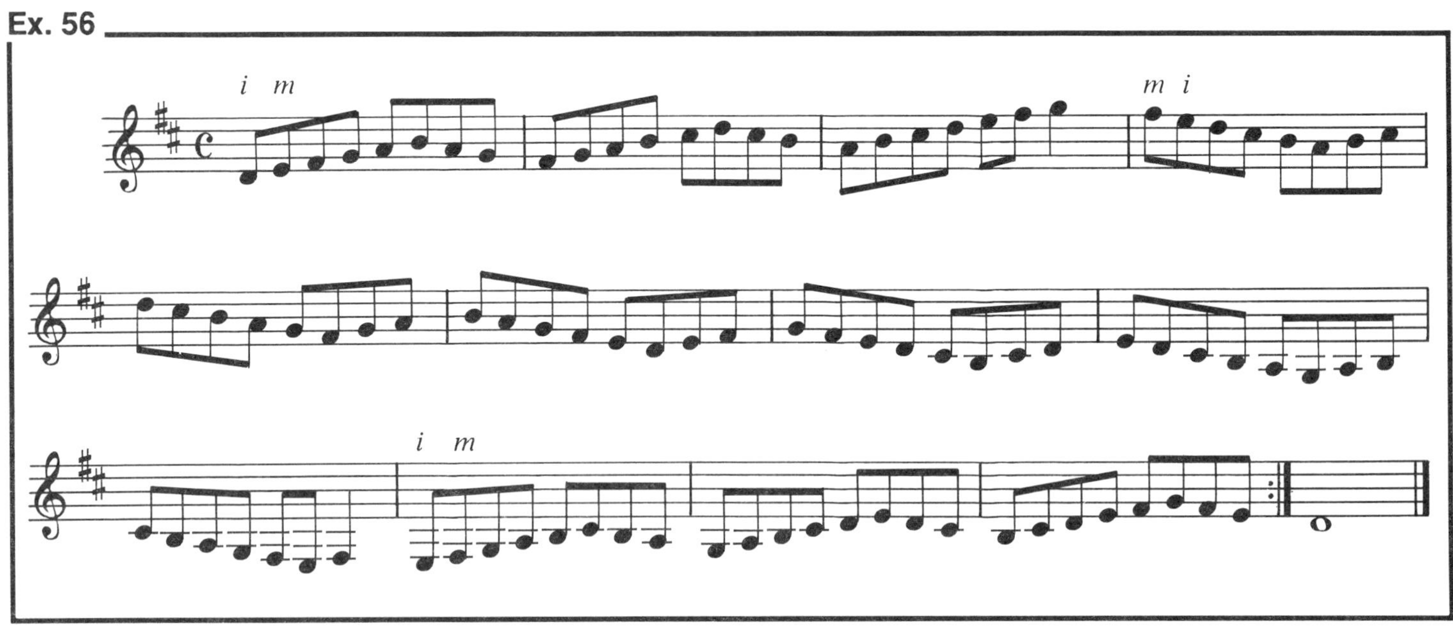

Ex. 57

Measure 8 of Duet 36 contains a hemiola rhythm — in this case, three pulses in a measure of compound duple meter. Since the largest common subdivision is the eighth, you should count measure 8 as follows:

1 & 2 & 3 &

(This page is left blank to avoid a page turn in the following piece.)

Duet No. 36

Saltarello

A. H.

M.M. ♩. = 80+

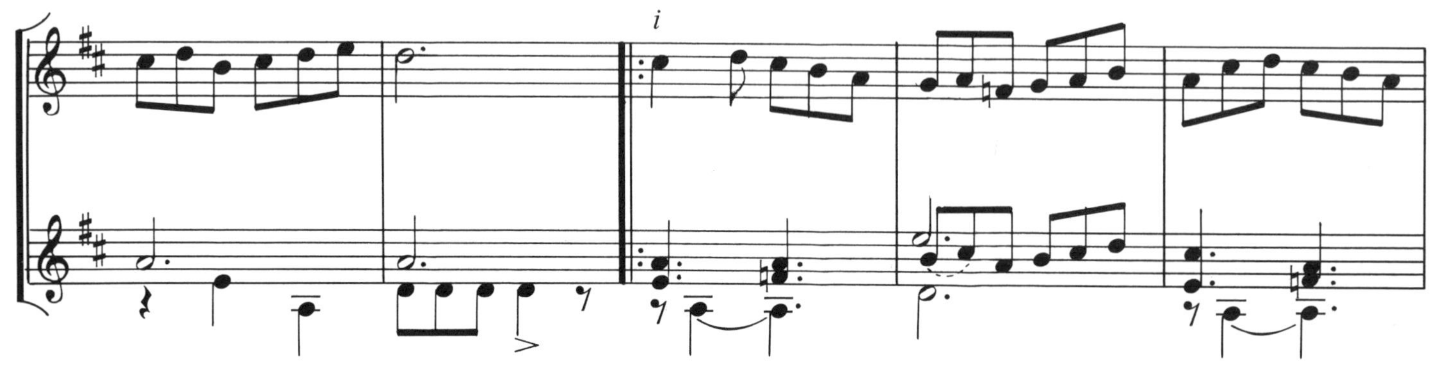

i
3
i
i

Soliloquy

Solo No. 47

A. H.

(This page is left blank to avoid a page turn in the following piece.)

In Duet 37, carefully observe the E♯(My) on ① at I, which you've previously read as F♮. Also observe the B♯(Tie) on ② at I, which you've previously read as C♮.

Accidental Melody

Duet No. 37

A. H.

BIII ②
BII
BIII
poco rit.
a tempo
rit.

Solos No. 48 and No. 49 introduce a, m, i, m — the third of the five arpeggios without p. *Again, before you begin to play, be sure you clearly understand the finger movements involved in this arpeggio.* You'll find an explanation of this arpeggio in *Part One*, p. 103.

Solo No. 48

A, M, I, M Etude I

A. H.

Solo No. 49

A, M, I, M Etude II

A. S.

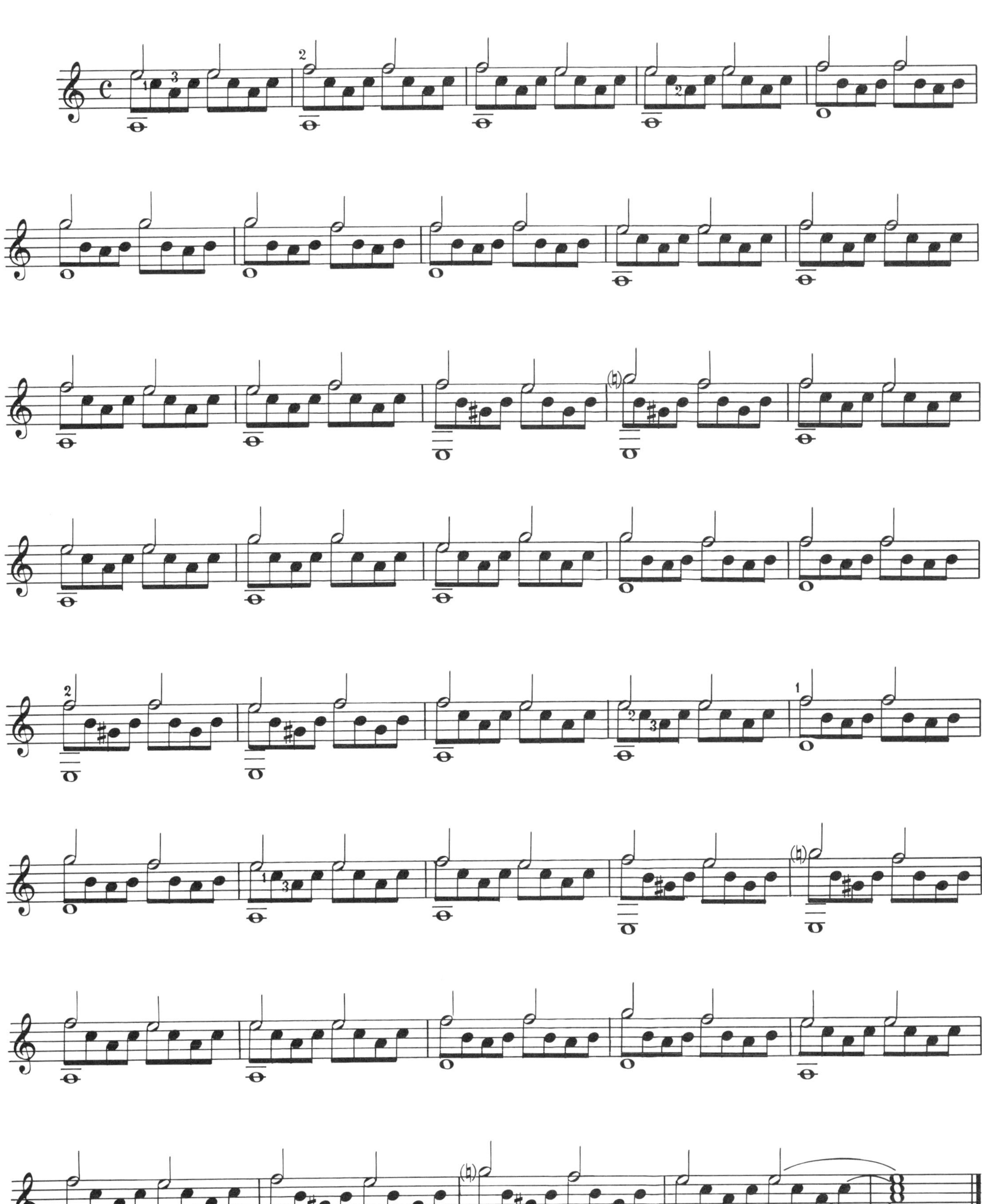

The Complete Open-Position Chromatic Scale

A chromatic scale consists entirely of half steps and requires the frequent use of chromatic signs. The ***Complete Open-Position Chromatic Scale*** extends from the open ⑥, E (Mi), to G♯ (Si) on ①. This scale encompasses the open strings and the first four frets of each string (except ③, which requires only three frets in the chromatic scale). Either sharps or flats can be used exclusively in notating a chromatic scale. For ease in reading, however, sharps are used when the scale ascends and flats are used when the scale descends.

When playing, place each left-hand finger close to its fret, giving special attention to your third and fourth fingers. To avoid unnecessary opposed movements between adjacent fingers when playing an ascending scale, gently hold each finger on the string until proceeding to the next higher string. In descending, place each finger only as needed. Memorize Ex. 58 through visualization.

Ex. 58

Because it uses all four fingers, the complete open-position chromatic scale is extremely beneficial as a technical exercise. You should practice it daily.

Duet No. 38 is based on the early jazz style of piano playing called "boogie-woogie." This piece provides practice in reading accidentals, and it also provides further training for the third and fourth fingers. Since your fingers naturally draw together when flexed and move sideways more easily when extended, the frets on the lower strings are easier to reach with 3 and 4 than the same frets on the higher strings.

As usual, thoroughly carry out the Pre-Reading Procedure before playing. Be sure to observe the B♯ (Tie) on ⑤ at III, which you've previously read as C♮. Then begin to play slowly and accurately. Isolate and practice any troublesome passages until you can do them with ease.

If you're playing at a slow tempo, use p. To play at a faster tempo, alternate m and i, beginning each measure with m.

Boogie-Woogie Blues

S - H

M.M. ♩= 104+

Solo No. 50

Divertimento

A. H.

The Complete Open-Position A-Major Scale Form

The ***Complete Open-Position A-Major Scale Form*** includes A (La) on the first string at V, notated on the first ledger line above the staff. The key signature consists of the three sharps: F♯, C♯, and G♯. To execute this scale, you must shift your left hand (including the thumb) the distance of one fret, forming F♯ (Fi) on ① at II with 1, G♯ (Si) with 3, and A with 4. The remaining notes of the scale on the other five strings are played in open position, with 1 covering I and the other three fingers covering frets II, III, and IV.

Practice Ex. 59 until you can comfortably play the two new notes, G♯ and A. Then practice Ex. 60. Notice that, since both shifts are done while you sound the open first string, you can easily shift to the second position and back.

When you can play Ex. 60 smoothly and confidently, memorize and practice the complete open-position A-major scale form (Ex. 61).

Ex. 59

Ex. 60

Ex. 61

Ex. 62 (Scale Exercise)

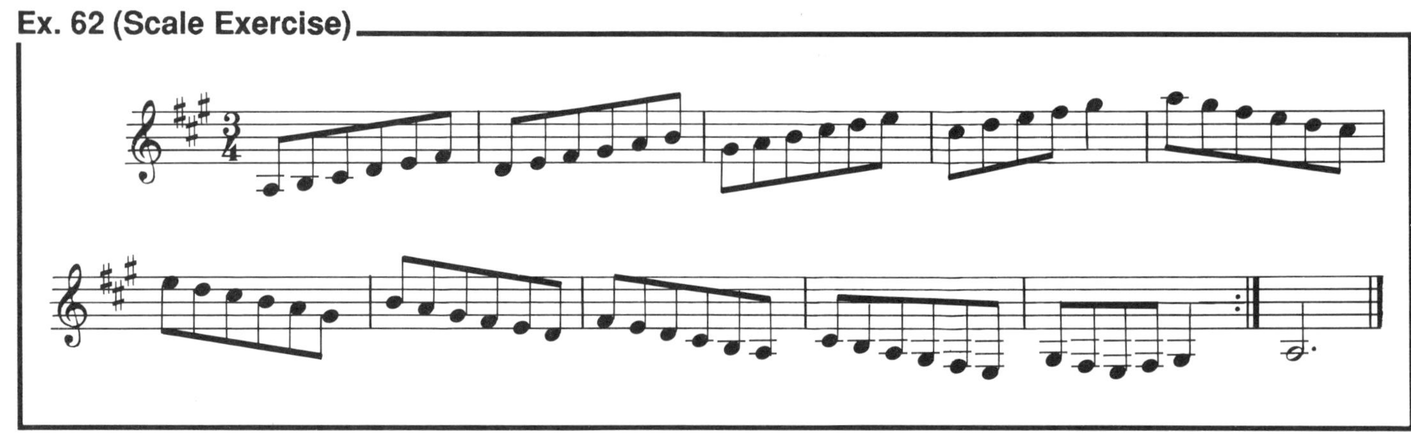

In Solo No. 51, notice that some notes are marked as follows: ♩̇ . A dot placed directly above a note is the sign for ***staccato*** (Italian, pronounced "stah-**cah**-toh"). Staccato means to discreetly shorten the note or chord over which the dot appears.

Notice also that some notes are marked as follows: > . This is an ***accent mark,*** which indicates that the note or chord over which it appears should be played more loudly.

Solo No. 51

Quint-Waltz

A. H.

M.M. ♩ = 112+

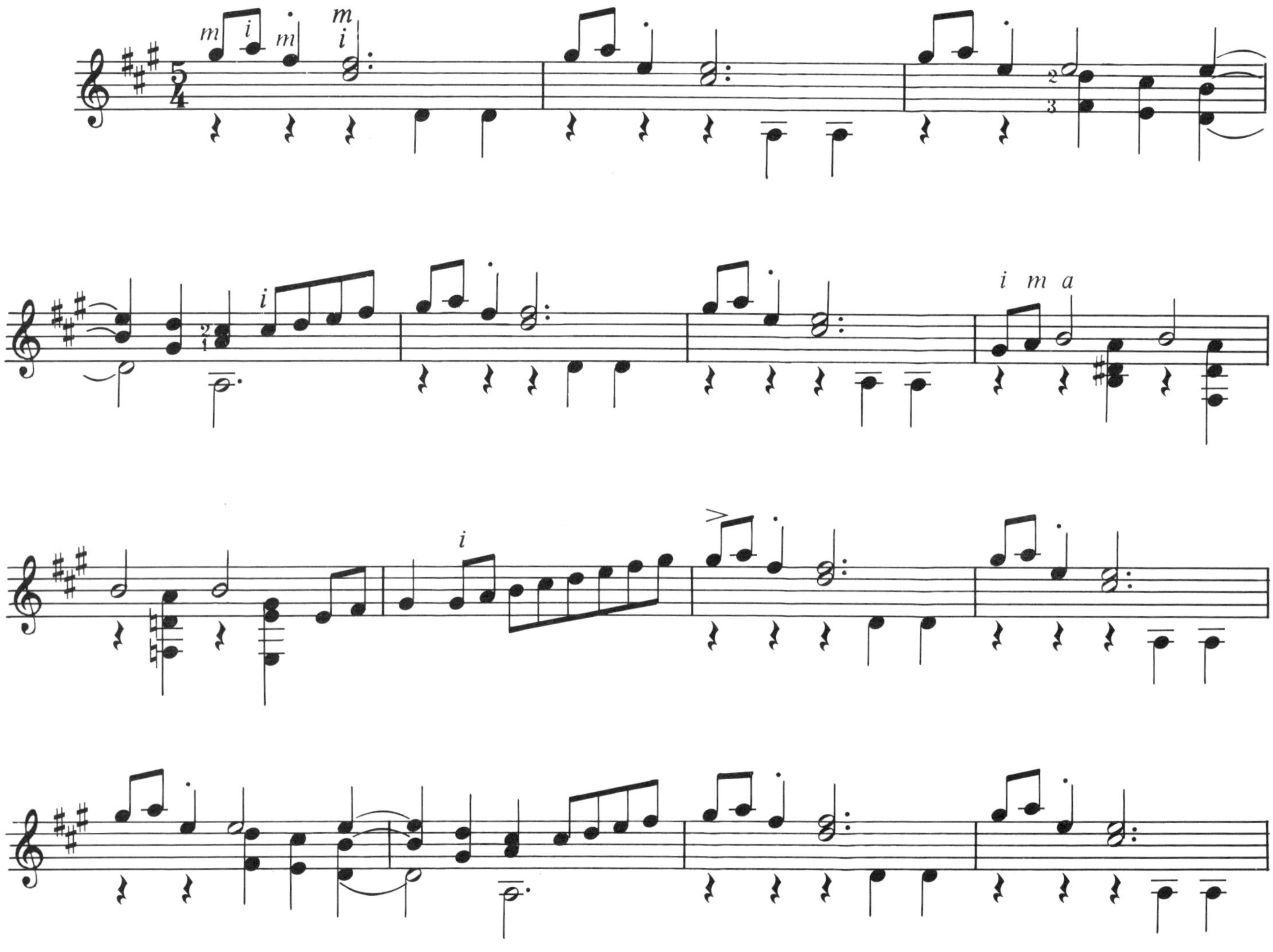

m i
m i
i m
m
i
p-
i m a
m i

Solo No. 52

Reverie

A. H.

M.M. ♩ = 76+

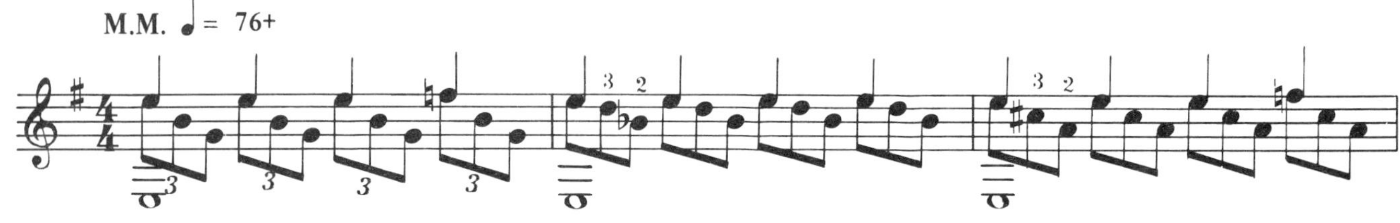

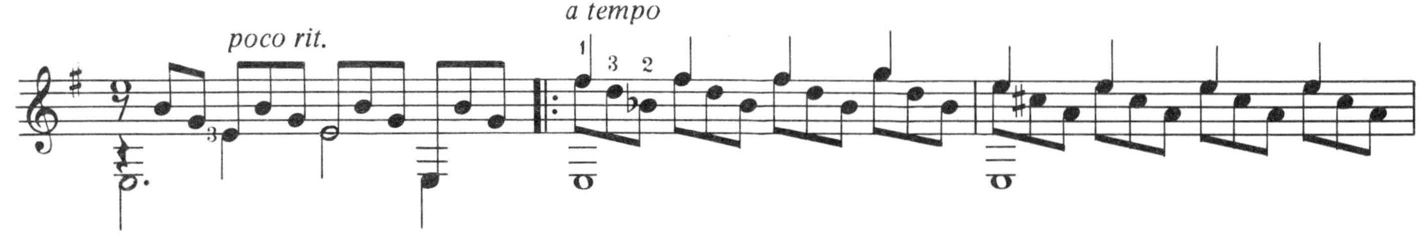

Habañera

Duet No. 39

A. H.

1.
2.

Solo No. 53 introduces i, a, m, a — the fourth of the five arpeggios without p. Again, before you begin to play, be sure you clearly understand the finger movements involved in this arpeggio. You'll find an explanation of this arpeggio in *Part One*, p. 104.

Be sure to observe the B (Ti) on ③ at IV (measure 3).

Solo No. 53

I, A, M, A Etude

A. H.

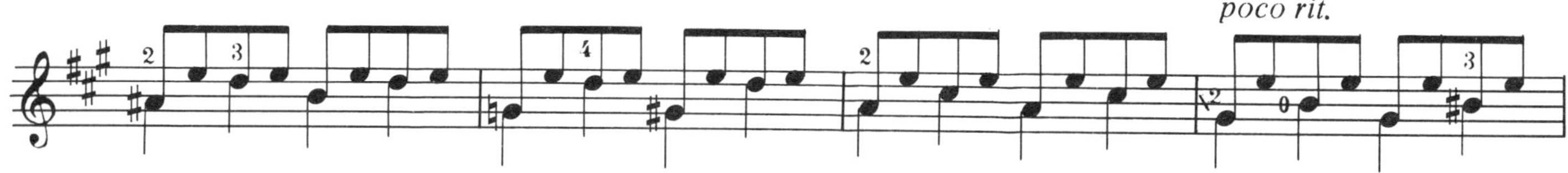

poco rit.
a tempo

The Complete Open-Position E-Major Scale Form

Ex. 63

Ex. 64 (Scale Exercise)

Until now, you've encountered mixed-meter pieces in which only the undotted value represents the beat. Solo No. 54, however, contains alternating measures of 6/8 and 2/4. This means that you'll now count music in which the beat is alternately represented by a dotted and an undotted value.

Your approach to counting this piece should be similar to the approach for counting hemiola (see p. 143). Thus, you'll count Solo No. 54 by using the eighth value — the largest subdivision common to both 6/8 and 2/4:

(This page is left blank to avoid a page turn in the following piece.)

Danza Mexicana

Solo No. 54

A. H.

3

Duet No. 40

Gavotte

A. H.

BII
BII
1.
2.
rit.

Solo No. 55 introduces a, i, m, i — the last of the five arpeggios without p. You'll find an explanation of this arpeggio in *Part One*, p. 105.

Solo No. 55

A, I, M, I Etude

A. H.

Humoreske

Duet No. 41

A. H.

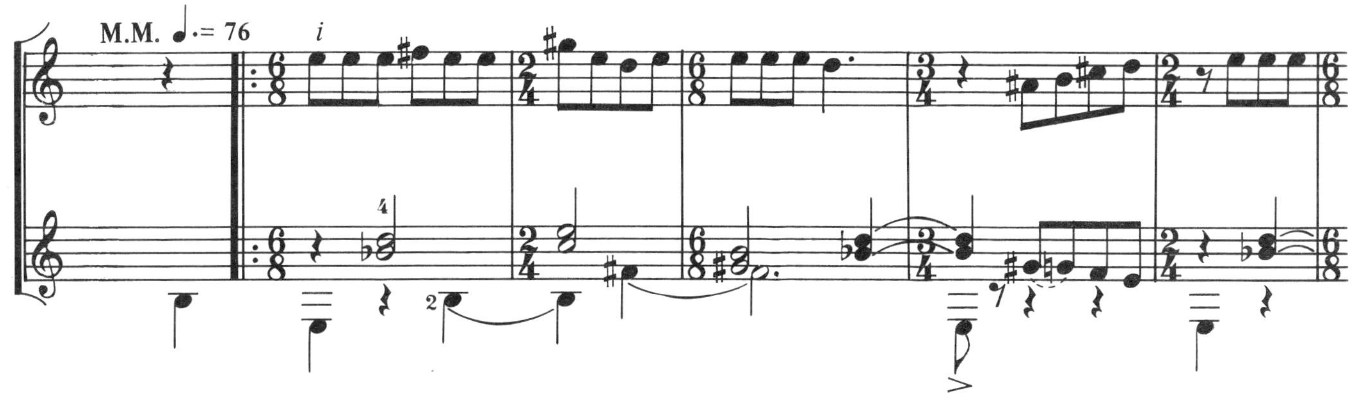

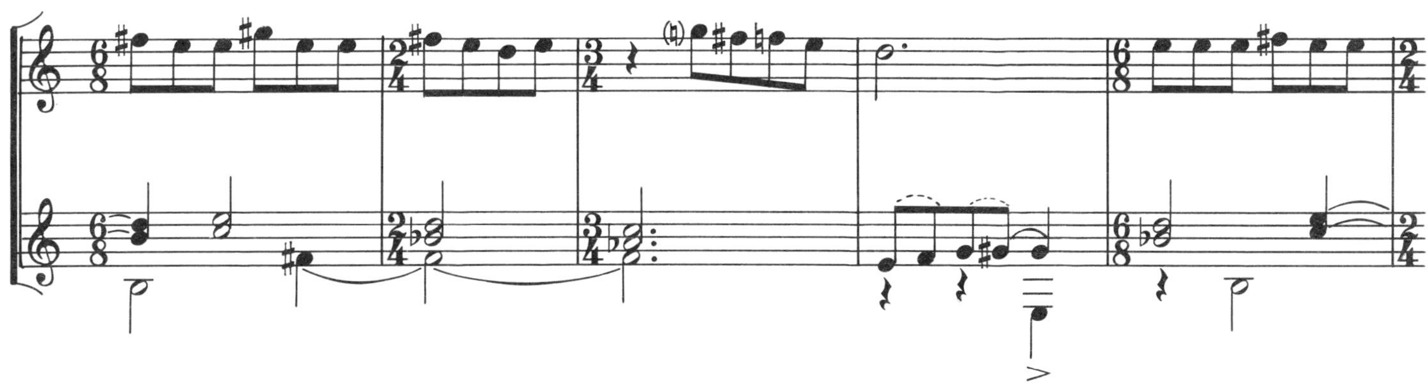

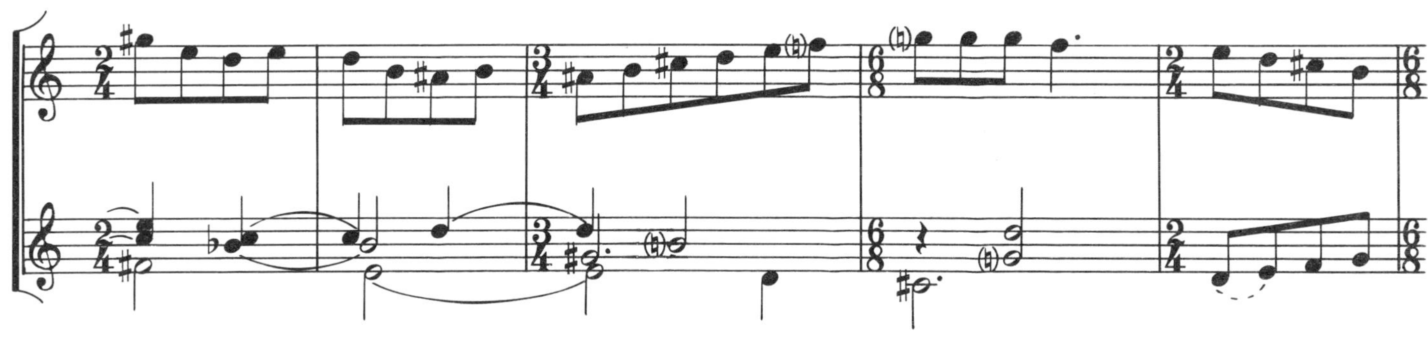

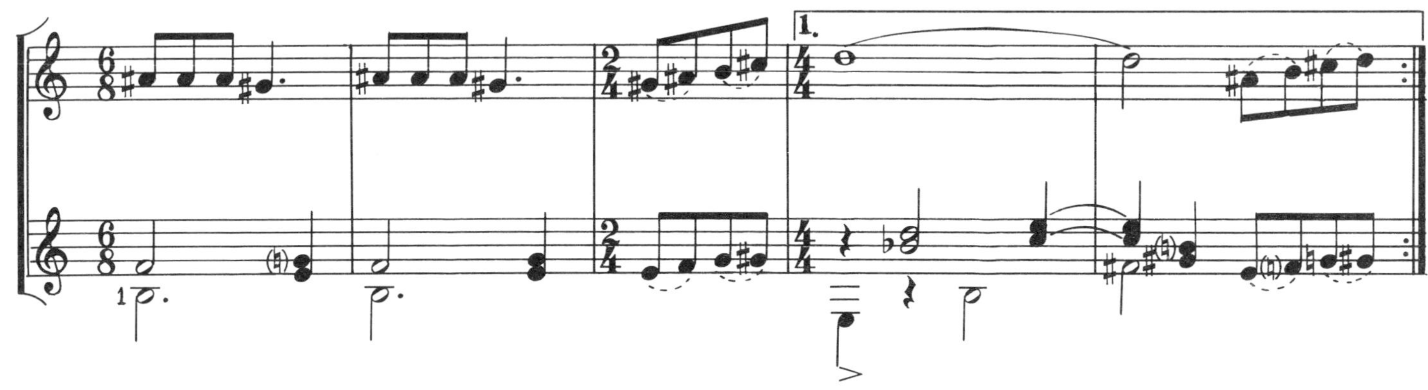

2.
m
m
2
3 0 2 4

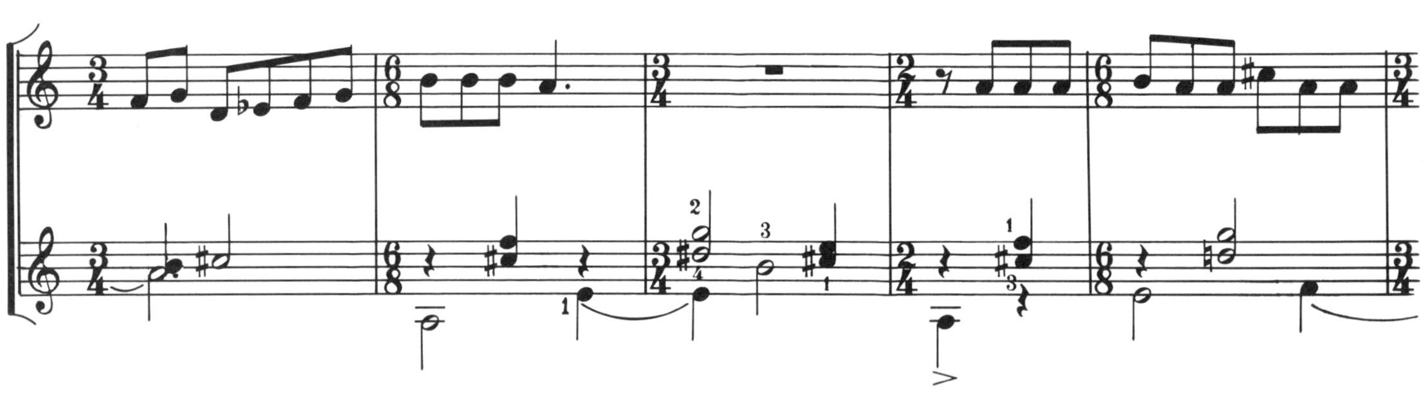
2
3
1
1
1
3

poco rit.
a tempo

Solo No. 56

Carousel

A. H.

M.M. ♩. = 58+

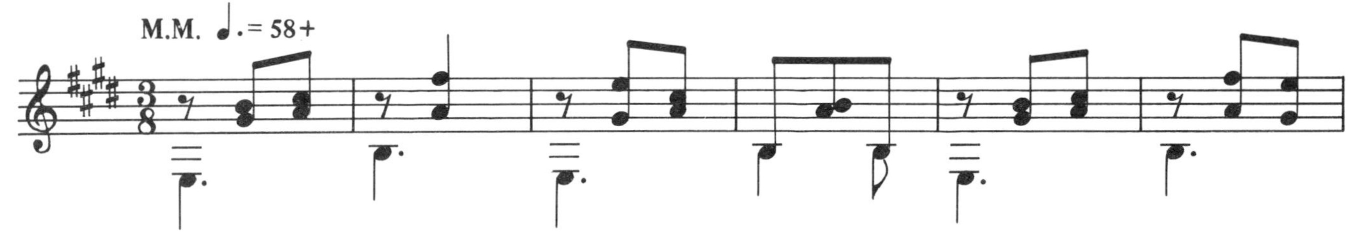

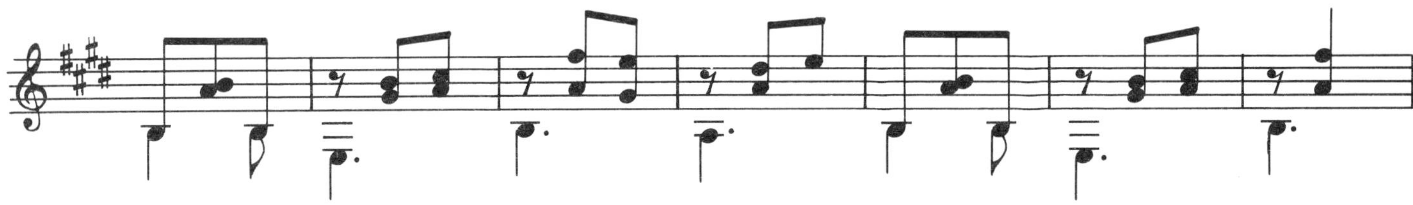

rit.
a tempo
1.
2.

String Damping

String damping is the act of deliberately touching one or more strings to stop their vibration. One obvious application for damping is to observe musical rests:

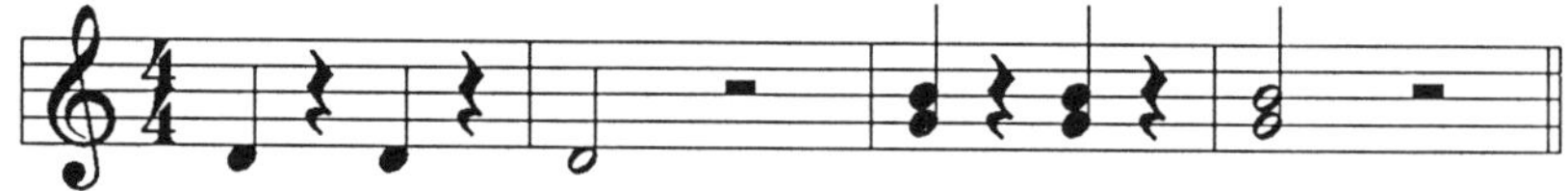

There are other situations, however, where damping is necessary. When a guitar string is sounded, unless damped, it will continue to sound until its vibration gradually dies out. This can cause problems in a musical context, as illustrated in the following musical examples:

If the open E (Mi) and B (Ti) are allowed to sound past their written values, they'll clash with the notes which follow — this would blur the scalewise progression of notes.

If the second A (La) bass in the first measure is allowed to sound past its written value, it will clash with the harmony in the next measure. To avoid this, the A must be damped on the first beat of the second measure. Further, while there's no actual harmonic clash between measures 3 and 4, overlapping tones here would weaken the bass line.

Right-Hand Damping

There are three basic methods of right-hand damping:

- **Damping with the fingertips.**

- **Damping by placing the side of p̲ against all six strings. This is generally used to observe rests. It's also used to damp the strings at the conclusion of a piece.**

• **Damping individual strings with p. This is used when an individual note must be damped while other notes are sounding or being sounded. For example:**

The second A bass in the first measure must be damped as you sound the first beat of the following measure. You can do this by touching ⑤ with the tip of p. In measure 3, damp the E (Mi) bass with the side of p as you position p to sound ⑤.

Left-Hand Damping

There are three basic methods of left-hand damping:

• **Damping all six strings by lightly laying one or more fingers flat across the strings. Generally, this method is used only when it's inconvenient to damp with the right hand.**

• **Damping a string with an active finger. For example:**

The E must not be allowed to overlap the D. Damping with the right hand, however, would be needlessly awkward. A far simpler way is to lean 3 against ① as you form D (Re).

This technique is equally effective in bass passages. For example:

In the second measure, the open fifth string can easily be damped with 3 as it forms G (So).

• Damping a string with an inactive finger. This technique is particularly effective when the right hand is occupied with a fast passage. For example:

...as you form C♯ (Di) on ② with 2, you can damp ④ by lightly touching it with 3.

Damping with an inactive finger is also effective in cases when damping with the right hand would be extremely awkward. For example:

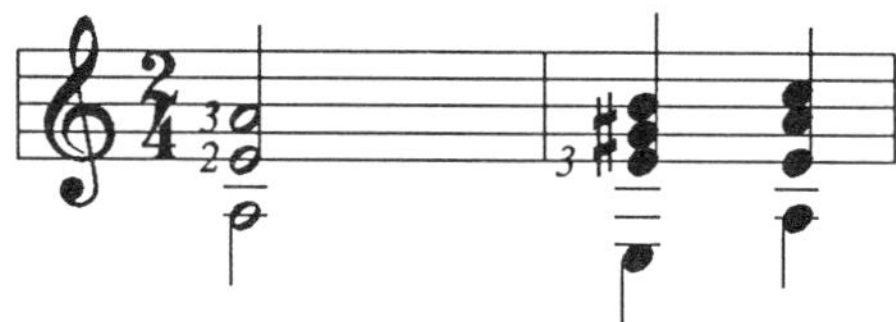

In the second measure, you can damp the open fifth string with 2, placing it as though you're playing a five-string E-major chord.

Solfege

Solfege refers to singing or speaking solmization syllables to name musical notes. There are two systems of solfege in common use. One system is called "Fixed Do" and consists of the syllables Do, Re, Mi, Fa, So, La, Si. These seven syllables represent both natural and chromatic notes. Thus, each syllable represents five different notes: the natural, its sharp and double sharp, and its flat and double flat.

The other system is called "Movable Do." In this system the tonic or key center is always Do. Thus, Do is relocated to conform with each key change throughout a piece. The same syllables are used (Do, Re, Mi, etc.), except that Si is replaced with Ti, and specific syllables are applied to chromatic notes.

Both these systems of solfege are used in teaching solfege or sight-singing. In sight-singing, you need only to sing the correct pitches — no further identification of the notes is needed. The demands of learning to play the guitar, however, differ considerably from the demands of sight-singing. The wide pitch range of guitar music often makes it impossible to sing. Further, it is essential that guitarists have a clear and permanent correlation between each printed note and its exact location on the guitar. Thus, whatever the merits of the Fixed-Do and Movable-Do systems in learning to sight-sing, neither is very useful in learning to play the guitar.

The Fixed-Do Chromatic Syllable System

A highly effective system of solfege for guitarists is the Fixed-Do Chromatic Syllable System. In this system, the note C is always Do and each note (including accidentals) has a distinct and permanent name:

Ascending with sharps:

Letter Name:	C	C♯	D	D♯	E	F	F♯	G	G♯	A	A♯	B	C
Syllable:	Do	Di	Re	Ri	Mi	Fa	Fi	So	Si	La	Li	Ti	Do
Pronounced:	Doh	Dee	Ray	Ree	Mee	Fah	Fee	Soh	See	Lah	Lee	Tee	Doh

E♯, B♯, and all double sharps are pronounced with an "ai": My, Tie, Die, Fie, etc.

Descending with Flats:

Letter Name:	C	B	B♭	A	A♭	G	G♭	F	E	E♭	D	D♭	C
Syllable:	Do	Ti	Te	La	Le	So	Se	Fa	Mi	Me	Re	Ra	Do
Pronounced:			Tay		Lay		Say			May		Rah	

C♭ and F♭ are pronounced with the usual "ay": Day, Fay. Double flats are pronounced with an "awe": Taw, Law, etc.

Ideally, you would have applied this system of solfege from the beginning of your guitar study. But even students who learn solfege later in their studies find it extremely beneficial. Learning solfege later, however, requires a certain steadfastness because you won't actually understand its benefits until you apply it in the memorization process.

The purpose of solfege is to realize written notes on the guitar. Thus, as you sing or say a syllable, always visualize its location on the guitar.

- ❑ **Solfege and visualize the open-position one-octave C-major scale on the guitar. *Be sure to associate each syllable with its exact location on the guitar.***

- ❑ **When you've clearly visualized the scale at an even and flowing tempo, play it on the guitar while continuing to name each solfege syllable aloud. Be keenly aware of the sound of each pitch as you solfege and play.**

- ❑ **When you're familiar with the scale, find an easy melodic piece in C major and memorize it through the memorization procedure outlined on pp. 213 – 220.**

As you become familiar with this application of solfege, you'll discover the following benefits:

• It provides a clear correlation of each note in the score with its location on the guitar.

• Musicians have long recognized the interpretive benefits of singing a melodic line whenever possible. This system affords a practical way to accurately identify each pitch as you sing.

• Properly applied in memorization, each syllable prompts an instant recall of the note's pitch, its location on the guitar, and the fingering for both hands. On advanced levels, it helps you discern how each note fits into the interpretive scheme of the composition.

• Verbalizing syllables helps you pinpoint deficiencies in your memorization of a piece.

• *Verbalizing syllables and visualizing them on the guitar helps you to develop the sustained concentration essential for playing and performing music.* This is one of the most important benefits of solfege. Since you always correlate each syllable with its location on the guitar, solfege gives you definite images to concentrate on as you memorize music. Further, visualizing the syllables in correct rhythm demands sustained concentration.

When you're familiar with the key of C major, you should gradually learn all the flat and sharp keys in the same manner. Begin with G major (the key of one sharp), then F major (one flat), then D major (two sharps), then B♭ major (two flats), etc. Visualize each scale before playing it, then play the scale while solfeging aloud. If possible, sing each syllable as you play. When you become reasonably adept at solfege, begin applying it in the memorization of simple pieces.

Summary

Always remember that the purpose of solfege is to realize written notes on the guitar—as you speak or sing a solfege syllable, you should always visualize its location on the guitar.

With careful and consistent application, solfege will help you become a more accurate and confident performer. Review all material in this book—even if you already read music. Be alert to any weaknesses in your ability both to identify written notes by their solfege syllables and to correlate their location on the guitar.

Memorizing Music

Memorization is an essential skill for any aspiring guitarist. No matter how secure your technique, you won't be a secure performer until you can confidently memorize music. Although some people memorize more readily than others, memorization doesn't require special talent. If you can learn to read and play simple pieces, you can also learn to memorize and perform music confidently.

Like every other aspect of guitar study, secure memorization is an acquired skill. To acquire this skill, you must avoid confusion and error when reading and playing music on the guitar. If you're confused and making errors when reading a piece, then that's exactly what you'll memorize — confusion and error will become part of your playing.

Eliminating Confusion and Error

Confusion is caused by a lack of understanding. Perhaps you're unfamiliar with certain areas of the fingerboard, or you haven't mastered a complex rhythm. Or maybe you haven't sufficiently studied a challenging fingering. Whatever the reason, the result is certain: Confusion disrupts your concentration, causing you either to make errors or feel you're about to make errors. This, of course, destroys your security and confidence.

Fortunately, you can avoid confusion by carefully selecting and examining the music you're about to study. By isolating and studying problem passages separately, you can clarify any unfamiliar pitches, complex rhythms, or awkward fingerings.

Thus, since confusion is avoidable, most errors are also avoidable. Through careful preparation, you can reduce confusion to a minimum, and you can often avoid it altogether.

Most students give insufficient attention to confusion and error when learning a new piece. They assume they can eliminate errors after memorizing the piece. Thus, they develop powerful habits of error which they must laboriously try to correct. Students who try to eliminate errors after memorizing a piece never perform as securely and confidently as they could if they had developed habits of accuracy from the beginning.

When approaching a new piece for study, how soon should you begin eliminating confusion and error? The answer is simple: ***You should eliminate confusion and error before beginning to play the piece. You automatically begin memorizing from your first reading, and this memorization tends to stick a little longer each time you play. Thus, from the first reading, you should establish habits of accuracy, continuity, and confidence.***

Selecting Music for Study

Since you'll be dealing with rhythms, pitches, and fingerings, you need to carefully consider the complexity of the music you select. If you choose music which is too complex for your level of development, you'll either experience confusion and error, or you'll have to work extremely slowly to avoid them. Both are undesirable. ***Always select a piece which, with reasonable preparation, you can read and play without confusion and error.***

You should evaluate a new piece through the following procedure:

- ❑ **Scan the piece for rhythm problems. Are there any rhythmic figures which you don't understand? If so, will you be able to solve them quickly?**
- ❑ **Scan the piece for pitch problems. Can you read all the pitches? Beware of long passages on unfamiliar areas of the fingerboard.**
- ❑ **Scan the piece for right- and left-hand difficulties. Does the piece contain fingering problems which you don't readily understand?**

∾ ∾ ∾ ∾ ∾ ∾ ∾

The purpose of this evaluation is to choose music that isn't too complex. For now, you should err on the side of caution when selecting music. Start with short and relatively simple pieces — pieces which allow you to concentrate on securely developing your reading and memorization skills.

Bear in mind, however, that the selection process doesn't necessarily end once you begin the memorization procedure. Sustained concentration is essential to the memorization procedure, and boredom is fatal to sustained concentration. Thus, be sensitive to boredom as you work with a piece. ***If you must study a piece for so long that you become consistently bored with it, then the piece isn't suitable for your present development.***

The Four-Step Memorization Procedure

You'll develop the ability to memorize music accurately and securely through the following procedure:

Step One: Pre-reading without the guitar.

Step Two: Reading and playing on the guitar.

Step Three: Testing your memorization without the guitar.

Step Four: Securing your memorization on the guitar.

CAUTION: If you rush through any one step, the entire procedure will collapse. Never go on to the next step until you can carry out the previous step with ease.

Step One: Pre-Reading without the Guitar

Memorization and reading are closely linked. How quickly you memorize depends upon your ability to accurately and securely read music. Guitarists who are good readers are almost always more fluent at memorization. The reason is simple: Good readers are seldom confused, make fewer errors, and thus build more accurate and secure habits.

At this point in your study, you should already be familiar with the Pre-Reading Procedure (see pp. 12–13 and p. 23). If you're beginning to work with longer and more complex pieces, however, you shouldn't attempt to pre-read too much material at once. The quickest and easiest way to work with a longer piece is to divide it into manageable segments. Thus, the Pre-Reading Procedure must now be adjusted to allow you to approach complex music without confusion.

If you're working with a relatively short and simple piece, you can go segment by segment through Steps One and Two through the entire piece. If you're working with a longer and more complex piece, you can divide it into musically logical sections and go through all four steps of the Memorization Procedure with each section.

Proceed as follows, *without the guitar:*

- ❑ **Carefully examine the music and decide how many measures you can handle without confusion and error. This will be the first segment. If the piece is long or complex, you may decide to take only the first few measures. If you understand phrasing, take a musically coherent group of notes or figures.† If the segment contains a particularly challenging figure, you may need to take only two or three notes at a time.**

- ❑ **Clarify each rhythmic figure within the segment by counting and directing the beat. As you count, determine the strong and weak beats within the segment. Finally, clap the rhythms as you count.**

†For an explanation of phrasing, see *Part Three.*

❑ **Now read and visualize the segment at a steady and meaningful tempo, as though you were playing it on the guitar. Count aloud, then solfege aloud as you visualize.† Repeat this step until you can easily and accurately visualize the segment.**

As you become adept at solfeging a single part, you can further clarify the texture of a piece by solfeging two or more parts in a slightly broken manner. The melody is solfeged on the beat, the other part(s) slightly before the beat:

Ex. a.

If the upper part is the melody: "me-do, re, do"

Ex. b.

If the lower part is the melody:

"do-me, fa, me"

When you've completed Step One with the first segment, you're ready to go on to Step Two. But before you do, ask yourself the following questions:

- **Have I carefully followed all the instructions within Step One?**
- **Can I do everything within this step with ease?**
- **Do I feel secure?**

Above all, be patient. You're developing the ability to focus and sustain your concentration — this is absolutely essential for reading and playing music on the guitar.

†For an explanation of solfege, see pp. 209 – 211.

Step Two: Reading and Playing on the Guitar

- ❑ **When you've clarified and solved all potential problems within the segment, immediately play it on the guitar. Play it slowly and without hesitation. First count aloud as you play the segment. Then solfege aloud as you play the segment. Apply the Aim-Directed Movement concept for moving your fingers on the guitar as you play.†**

- ❑ **Stop at the first sign of confusion. Be sensitive to errors as you play, but also be aware that some errors are more serious than others. If you occasionally miss or flub a note but don't hesitate, keep playing — you're building habits of continuity, so you shouldn't stop for a minor slip of the fingers. But if you hesitate before, during, or after an error, or if you repeatedly make the same error, you have a serious problem which demands immediate attention. Determine the cause of your confusion and use whatever part of the Pre-Reading Procedure necessary to solve the problem. *Hesitations or repeated errors always signal confusion — if you're confused, stop playing!***

When you can confidently play the segment without hesitation, you're ready to proceed to the next segment. Although you're not trying to memorize the piece at this point, bear in mind that you'll inevitably begin to memorize anything you play. Thus, to build secure habits of continuity, always work on the segments in order — don't skip back and forth through the piece. Again, be alert to the slightest sign of confusion! You're working to develop accuracy, continuity, and confidence — don't negate them by ignoring confusion and error.

When you reach the end of the piece or section, read and play it at a reasonable tempo. ***Repeat the entire piece or section as many times as necessary until you can play it securely and confidently.***

∾ ∾ ∾ ∾ ∾ ∾ ∾

As you read and visualize each segment in Step One, bear in mind that visualization isn't an end in itself. The only way to confirm your visualization in Step One is by immediately going to Step Two and playing the segment on the guitar. ***Thus, as soon as you can visualize a segment, immediately confirm it by accurately reading and playing it on the guitar.***

---

†For an explanation of aim-directed movement, see *Part One*, pp. 4 – 5.

If you have difficulty reading and playing the music you've selected, your problem may be one or more of the following:

- **You're trying to pre-read too much at once. Never try to pre-read more material than you can handle without confusion and error.**

- **Your study before playing wasn't thorough enough. Clear pre-reading is crucial. Be sure that you clarify all rhythms and fingerings. Don't try to play any material until you can visualize it with ease.**

- **The piece is too complex. You can select a piece with some technical challenges, but you should understand how to go about solving them. Again, never select a piece that you can't study without confusion and error.**

- **The tempo may be too fast. Always begin with a tempo that allows you to play with continuity and accuracy. Also, if the piece requires a fast tempo to be effective and you can't reach that tempo within a reasonable time, you should choose a less demanding piece.**

Whatever the reason, if you become even slightly confused as you try to play the music, *stop playing!* By trying to push stubbornly through confusion and error, you'll only ingrain extremely harmful habits.

Your aim in Step Two is to be able to play the piece or section without confusion and error. ***Thus, never go on to Steps Three and Four until you can securely and confidently play the piece or segment at a reasonable tempo.***

Step Three: Testing Your Memorization

By becoming thoroughly familiar with the music, you're well along the road to memorizing it. In fact, you may feel that you already have the entire piece or segment memorized, particularly if it's short and relatively simple. If you believe you have the piece or segment memorized, then the next step is to verify your memorization.

Never try to play music from memory until you've verified your memorization through careful visualization away from the guitar.

Proceed as follows:

- ❑ **Set both the guitar and music aside. Hold both hands in playing position as though you're playing an imaginary guitar. Now visualize while solfeging the most important line (generally the melody) and moving your fingers as though you're actually playing the piece — imagine your left hand at the fingerboard and your right hand sounding the strings.† You may find it easier to concentrate with your eyes closed. If necessary, shift your focus of concentration between hands, depending on which hand has the greater technical challenge. Proceed as slowly as necessary to avoid confusion and error.**

If you can accurately visualize the entire piece at least twice in succession, proceed to Step Four. (If you've broken the piece into smaller sections, you should be able to accurately visualize the entire section you're working on.) If you can't accurately visualize the piece (or section) in this manner, proceed as follows without the guitar:

Memorizing the Piece:

- ❑ **Using the visualization process, decide how far into the music you can securely visualize from memory. When you get to a point where you're uncertain of the next note, stop. Go back to the score and examine the problem passage. Select a musically logical phrase containing the problem passage.**

- ❑ **Memorize the rhythms by counting and clapping.**

- ❑ **Solfege the most important line — generally the melody. Read and visualize the segment several times, making sure that you can clearly imagine the music unfolding under your fingers. Then look away from the score and continue to visualize. Repeat until you feel you have the segment securely memorized.**

- ❑ **If you feel you've memorized the segment, test your memorization through the "Testing Your Memorization" procedure. If you can carry out this procedure with ease, proceed immediately to Step Four.**

∾ ∾ ∾ ∾ ∾ ∾ ∾

---

†Some teachers instruct their students to visualize the music itself, maintaining a mental image of the printed page. But reading a score — even a visualized score — is one step removed from realizing the music on the guitar. It's easier to play from memory by visualizing the piece as finger movements directly on the guitar rather than as notes on a page.

CAUTION: ***Once you've begun the memorization process, always study the music away from the guitar — never read and play at the same time.***

Remember, you're trying to securely memorize the music. If you continually play from the score, you're simply delaying the memorization process. Of course, there's no harm in going back and forth between the guitar and the score. Examine and visualize the music as often as necessary, and play each segment until you have it securely memorized. *But keep the score and the guitar separated — you'll memorize more quickly and securely.*

Step Four: Confirming Your Memorization

Play and repeat the piece or segment until you can confidently play it from memory. When memorizing by segments, develop continuity by always beginning to play from a point preceding each new segment. Continue in this manner until you reach the end of the piece or section.

At first, you may occasionally need to slow down or pause to recall a passage. As long as you hesitate deliberately and don't become confused, a hesitation or brief pause isn't harmful. But if you can't quickly recall the notes, or you find yourself grabbing for notes in a hit-or-miss fashion, you should set aside the guitar and return to "Memorizing the Piece" in Step Three (p. 218).

∾ ∾ ∾ ∾ ∾ ∾ ∾

As a final test of your memorization, carry out the following procedure with the guitar:

- ❑ **Play the first measure, then (without touching the strings) solfege and visualize the second measure, play the third measure, solfege and visualize the fourth, etc. Continue alternately playing and visualizing measure by measure without hesitation through the entire piece.**
- ❑ **When you reach the end of the piece or section, repeat the procedure, except this time begin by reversing the order — visualize the first measure, play the second, etc.**
- ❑ **Repeat this procedure until you can do it easily and securely.**

Summary

With patience and careful practice, you'll develop the ability to quickly and securely memorize even long and complex pieces. Further, this procedure helps you build a secure and enduring memory of music. Students often find that they can instantly recall and play a piece which they had learned months or even years before.

Always observe the following as you study and practice the memorization procedure:

• After visualizing and playing a new piece, don't expect that you'll necessarily be able to play it securely from memory a few hours later. In the beginning, you may need several reinforcement sessions of visualization and playing before you securely memorize a piece.

• Don't try to memorize too much or too quickly. Take whatever time you need to thoroughly analyze and learn the music. When you begin to work with longer and more complex pieces, you can memorize them in musically logical sections.

• Be flexible. There are some pieces which make certain parts of the memorization process impractical. For example, although solfege is extremely useful in clarifying the voicing of arpeggios, it's hardly practical to solfege every note of a rapid arpeggio at performance tempo. Instead, visualize the chord and its fingering. Then, if you're unfamiliar with the chord, play it to become acquainted with its sound. Use your knowledge of harmony to reinforce your memorization — identify each chord by name and harmonic function if you can.

Above all, be positive. Remember, learning to memorize is a challenging process. Your progress is directly affected by your attitude, so do not let minor setbacks destroy your confidence. Properly pursued, this memorization process is extremely rewarding.